CAMBRIDGE
UNIVERSITY PRESS

Biology

for Cambridge IGCSE™

EXAM PREPARATION AND PRACTICE

Alexander van Dijk and David Martindill

Contents

Practical guidance

Practical guidance and some digital questions can be found online at Cambridge GO.
For more information on how to access and use your digital resource, please see inside front cover.

> How to use this series

This suite of resources supports students and teachers following the Cambridge IGCSE Biology syllabus (0610). All of the components in the series are designed to work together and help students develop the necessary knowledge and skills for this subject. With clear language and style, they are designed for international students.

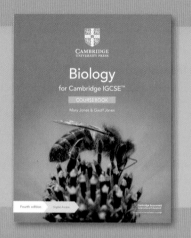

The coursebook provides coverage of the full Cambridge IGCSE™ Biology syllabus (0610). Each chapter explains facts and concepts and uses relevant real-world examples of scientific principles to bring the subject to life. Together with a focus on practical work and plenty of active learning opportunities, the coursebook prepares students for all aspects of their scientific study. Questions and exam-style questions in every chapter help students to consolidate their understanding and provide practice opportunities to apply their learning.

The teacher's resource contains detailed guidance for all topics of the syllabus, including common misconceptions identifying areas where students might need extra support, as well as an engaging bank of lesson ideas for each syllabus topic. Differentiation is emphasised with suggestions of appropriate interventions to support and stretch students. It also contains support for preparing and carrying out all the investigations in the practical workbook, including a set of sample results for when practicals aren't possible. Also included are scaffolded worksheets and unit tests for each chapter, as well as answers to all questions in every resource across this series.

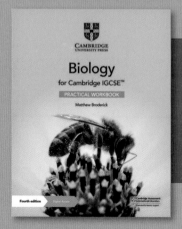

This workbook provides students with additional opportunities for hands-on practical work, giving them full guidance and support that will help them to develop their investigative skills. These skills include planning investigations, selecting and handling apparatus, creating hypotheses, recording and displaying results and analysing and evaluating data.

The skills-focused workbook has been constructed to help students develop the skills that they need as they progress through their Cambridge IGCSE™ Biology course, providing practice of all the topics in the coursebook. A three-tier, scaffolded approach to skills development enables students to progress through 'focus', 'practice' and 'challenge' exercises, ensuring that every student is supported.

Our research shows that English language skills are the single biggest barrier to students accessing international science. This write-in workbook contains exercises set within the context of Cambridge IGCSE™ Biology topics to consolidate understanding and embed practice in aspects of language central to the subject.

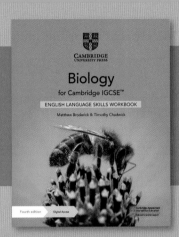

Mathematics is an integral part of scientific study and one that students often find a barrier to progression in science. The Maths Skills for Cambridge IGCSE™ Biology write-in workbook has been written in collaboration with the Association of Science Education, with each chapter focusing on several maths skills that their research concluded that students need to succeed in their Biology course.

The Exam Preparation and Practice resource provides dedicated support for students in preparing for their final assessments. Hundreds of questions in the book and accompanying digital resource will help students to check that they understand and can recall, syllabus concepts. To help students to show what they know in an exam context, a specially developed framework of exam skills with corresponding questions and past paper question practice, is also included. Self-assessment and reflection features support students to identify any areas that need further practice. This resource should be used alongside the coursebook, throughout the course of study, so students can most effectively increase their confidence and readiness for their exams.

> How to use this book

This book will help you to check that you **know** the content of the syllabus and practise how to **show** this understanding in an exam. It will also help you be cognitively prepared and in the **flow**, ready for your exam. Research has shown that it is important that you do all three of these things, so we have designed the Know, Show, Flow approach to help you prepare effectively for exams.

| Know | You will need to consolidate and then recall a lot of syllabus content. |

| Show | You should demonstrate your knowledge in the context of a Cambridge exam. |

| Flow | You should be cognitively engaged and ready to learn. This means reducing test anxiety. |

Exam skills checklist

Category	Exam skill
Understanding the question	Recognise different question types
	Understand command words
	Mark scheme awareness
Providing an appropriate response	Understand connections between concepts
	Keep to time
	Know what a good answer looks like
Developing supportive behaviours	Reflect on progress
	Manage test anxiety

This **Exam skills checklist** helps you to develop the awareness, behaviours and habits that will support you when revising and preparing for your exams. For more exam skills advice, including understanding command words and managing your time effectively, please go to the **Exam skills chapter**.

Know

The full syllabus content of your IGCSE Biology course is covered in your Cambridge coursebook. This book will provide you with different types of questions to support you as you prepare for your exams. You will answer **Knowledge recall questions** that are designed to make sure you understand a topic, and **Recall and connect questions** to help you recall past learning and connect different concepts.

KNOWLEDGE FOCUS

Knowledge focus boxes summarise the topics that you will answer questions on in each chapter of this book. You can refer back to your Cambridge coursebook to remind yourself of the full detail of the syllabus content.

You will find **Knowledge recall questions** to make sure you understand a topic, and **Recall and connect questions** to help you recall past learning and connect different concepts. It is recommended that you answer the Knowledge recall questions just after you have covered the relevant topic in class, and then return to them at a later point to check you have properly understood the content.

Knowledge recall questions

Testing yourself is a good way to check that your understanding is secure. These questions will help you to recall the core knowledge you have acquired during your course, and highlight any areas where you may need more practice. They are indicated with a blue bar with a gap, at the side of the page. We recommend that you answer the Knowledge recall questions just after you have covered the relevant topic in class, and then return to them at a later point to check you have properly understood the content.

≪ RECALL AND CONNECT ≪

To consolidate your learning, you need to test your memory frequently. These questions will test that you remember what you learned in previous chapters, in addition to what you are practising in the current chapter.

UNDERSTAND THESE TERMS

These list the important vocabulary that you should understand for each chapter. Definitions are provided in the glossary of your Cambridge coursebook.

Show

Exam questions test specific knowledge, skills and understanding. You need to be prepared so that you have the best opportunity to show what you know in the time you have during the exam. In addition to practising recall of the syllabus content, it is important to build your exam skills throughout the year.

EXAM SKILLS FOCUS

This feature outlines the exam skills you will practise in each chapter, alongside the Knowledge focus. They are drawn from the core set of eight exam skills, listed in the Exam skills checklist. You will practise specific exam skills, such as understanding command words, within each chapter. More general exam skills, such as managing text anxiety, are covered in the Exam skills chapter.

Exam skills questions

These questions will help you to develop your exam skills and demonstrate your understanding. To help you become familiar with exam-style questioning, many of these questions follow the style and use the language of real exam questions, and have allocated marks. They are indicated with a solid red bar at the side of the page.

Looking at sample answers to past paper questions helps you to understand what to aim for.

The **Exam practice** sections in this resource contain example student responses and examiner-style commentary showing how the answer could be improved (both written by the authors).

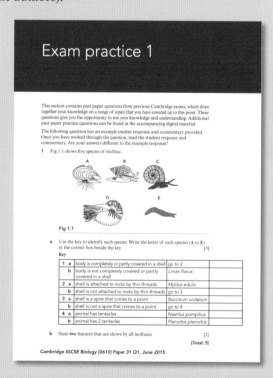

Supplement content

Where content is intended for students who are studying the Supplement content of the syllabus as well as the Core, this is indicated using the arrow and the bar, as on the left here. Supplement questions in the accompanying digital material are flagged in the question titles.

Flow

Preparing for exams can be stressful. One of the approaches recommended by educational psychologists to help with this stress is to improve behaviours around exam preparation. This involves testing yourself in manageable chunks, accompanied by self-evaluation. You should avoid cramming and build in more preparation time. This book is structured to help you do this.

Increasing your ability to recognise the signs of exam-related stress and working through some techniques for how to cope with it will help to make your exam preparation manageable.

REFLECTION

This feature asks you to think about the approach that you take to your exam preparation, and how you might improve this in the future. Reflecting on how you plan, monitor and evaluate your revision and preparation will help you to do your best in your exams.

SELF-ASSESSMENT CHECKLIST

These checklists return to the learning intentions from your coursebook, as well as the Exam skills focus boxes from each chapter. Checking in on how confident you feel in each of these areas will help you to focus your exam preparation. The 'Show it' prompts will allow you to test your rating. You should revisit any areas that you rate 'Needs more work' or 'Almost there'.

Now I can:	Show it	Needs more work	Almost there	Confident to move on

Increasing your ability to recognise the signs of exam-related stress and working through some techniques for how to cope with it will help to make your exam preparation manageable. The **Exam skills chapter** will support you with this.

Digital support

Extra self-assessment knowledge questions for all chapters can be found online at Cambridge GO. For more information on how to access and use your digital resource, please see inside the front cover.

You will find **Answers** for all of the questions in the book on the 'supporting resources' area of the Cambridge GO platform.

Multiple choice questions

These ask you to select the correct answer to a question from four options. These are auto-marked and feedback is provided.

Flip card questions

These present a question on one screen, and suggested answers on the reverse.

Syllabus assessment objectives for IGCSE Biology

You should be familiar with the Assessment Objectives from the syllabus, as the examiner will be looking for evidence of these requirements in your responses and allocating marks accordingly.

The assessment objectives for this syllabus are:

Assessment objective	Weighting
AO1: Knowledge with understanding	50%
AO2: Handling information and problem-solving	30%
AO3: Experimental skills and investigations	20%

Exam skills

by Lucy Parsons

What's the point of this book?

Most students make one really basic mistake when they're preparing for exams. What is it? It's focusing far too much on learning 'stuff' – that's facts, figures, ideas, information – and not nearly enough time practising exam skills.

The students who work really, really hard but are disappointed with their results are nearly always students who focus on memorising stuff. They think to themselves, 'I'll do practice papers once I've revised everything.' The trouble is, they start doing practice papers too late to really develop and improve how they communicate what they know.

What could they do differently?

When your final exam script is assessed, it should contain specific language, information and thinking skills in your answers. If you read a question in an exam and you have no idea what you need to do to give a good answer, the likelihood is that your answer won't be as brilliant as it could be. That means your grade won't reflect the hard work you've put into revising for the exam.

There are different types of questions used in exams to assess different skills. You need to know how to recognise these question types and understand what you need to show in your answers.

So, how do you understand what to do in each question type?

That's what this book is all about. But first a little background.

Meet Benjamin Bloom

The psychologist Benjamin Bloom developed a way of classifying and valuing different skills we use when we learn, such as analysis and recalling information. We call these thinking skills. It's known as Bloom's Taxonomy and it's what most exam questions are based around.

If you understand Bloom's Taxonomy, you can understand what any type of question requires you to do. So, what does it look like?

Bloom's Taxonomy of thinking skills

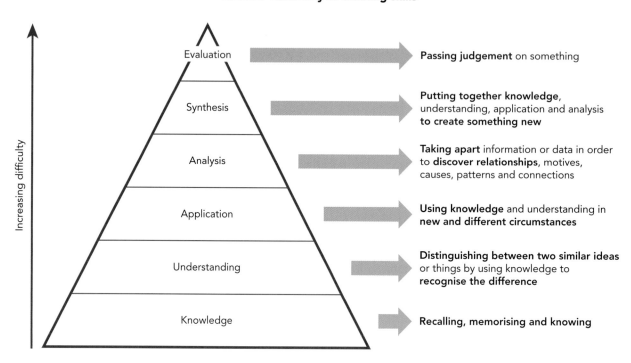

The key things to take away from this diagram are:

- Knowledge and understanding are known as lower-level thinking skills. They are less difficult than the other thinking skills. Exam questions that just test you on what you know are usually worth the lowest number of marks.

- All the other thinking skills are worth higher numbers of marks in exam questions. These questions need you to have some foundational knowledge and understanding but are far more about how you think than what you know. They involve:

  - Taking what you know and using it in unfamiliar situations (application).

  - Going deeper into information to discover relationships, motives, causes, patterns and connections (analysis).

  - Using what you know and think to create something new – whether that's an essay, long-answer exam question a solution to a maths problem, or a piece of art (synthesis).

  - Assessing the value of something, e.g. the reliability of the results of a scientific experiment (evaluation).

In this introductory chapter, you'll be shown how to develop the skills that enable you to communicate what you know and how you think. This will help you achieve to the best of your abilities. In the rest of the book, you'll have a chance to practise these exam skills by understanding how questions work and understanding what you need to show in your answers.

Every time you pick up this book and do a few questions, you're getting closer to achieving your dream results. So, let's get started!

Exam preparation and revision skills

What is revision?

If you think about it, the word 'revision' has two parts to it:

- re – which means 'again'

- vision – which is about seeing.

So, revision is literally about 'seeing again'. This means you're looking at something that you've already learned.

Typically, a teacher will teach you something in class. You may then do some questions on it, write about it in some way, or even do a presentation. You might then have an end-of-topic test sometime later. To prepare for this test, you need to 'look again' or revise what you were originally taught.

Step 1: Making knowledge stick

Every time you come back to something you've learned or revised you're improving your understanding and memory of that particular piece of knowledge. This is called **spaced retrieval**. This is how human memory works. If you don't use a piece of knowledge by recalling it, you lose it.

Everything we learn has to be physically stored in our brains by creating neural connections – joining brain cells together. The more often we 'retrieve' or recall a particular piece of knowledge, the stronger the neural connection gets. It's like lifting weights – the more often you lift, the stronger you get.

However, if you don't use a piece of knowledge for a long time, your brain wants to recycle the brain cells and use them for another purpose. The neural connections get weaker until they finally break, and the memory has gone. This is why it's really important to return often to things that you've learned in the past.

Great ways of doing this in your revision include:

- Testing yourself using flip cards – use the ones available in the digital resources for this book.

- Testing yourself (or getting someone else to test you) using questions you've created about the topic.

- Checking your recall of previous topics by answering the Recall and connect questions in this book.

- Blurting – writing everything you can remember about a topic on a piece of paper in one colour. Then, checking what you missed out and filling it in with another colour. You can do this over and over again until you feel confident that you remember everything.

- Answering practice questions – use the ones in this book.

- Getting a good night's sleep to help consolidate your learning.

> **The importance of sleep and creating long-term memory**
>
> When you go to sleep at night, your brain goes through an important process of taking information from your short-term memory and storing it in your long-term memory.
>
> This means that getting a good night's sleep is a very important part of revision. If you don't get enough good quality sleep, you'll actually be making your revision much, much harder.

Step 2: Developing your exam skills

We've already talked about the importance of exam skills, and how many students neglect them because they're worried about covering all the knowledge.

What actually works best is developing your exam skills at the same time as learning the knowledge.

What does this look like in your studies?

- Learning something at school and your teacher setting you questions from this book or from past papers. This tests your recall as well as developing your exam skills.

- Choosing a topic to revise, learning the content and then choosing some questions from this book to test yourself at the same time as developing your exam skills.

The reason why practising your exam skills is so important is that it helps you to get good at communicating what you know and what you think. The more often you do that, the more fluent you'll become in showing what you know in your answers.

Step 3: Getting feedback

The final step is to get feedback on your work.

If you're testing yourself, the feedback is what you got wrong or what you forgot. This means you then need to go back to those things to remind yourself or improve your understanding. Then, you can test yourself again and get more feedback. You can also congratulate yourself for the things you got right – it's important to celebrate any success, big or small.

If you're doing past paper questions or the practice questions in this book, you will need to mark your work. Marking your work is one of the most important things you can do to improve. It's possible to make significant improvements in your marks in a very short space of time when you start marking your work.

Why is marking your own work so powerful? It's because it teaches you to identify the strengths and weaknesses of your own work. When you look at the mark scheme and see how it's structured, you will understand what is needed in your answers to get the results you want.

This doesn't just apply to the knowledge you demonstrate in your answers. It also applies to the language you use and whether it's appropriately subject-specific, the structure of your answer, how you present it on the page and many other factors. Understanding, practising and improving on these things are transformative for your results.

The most important thing about revision

The most important way to make your revision successful is to make it active.

Sometimes, students say they're revising when they sit staring at their textbook or notes for hours at a time. However, this is a really ineffective way to revise because it's passive. In order to make knowledge and skills stick, you need to be doing something like the suggestions in the following diagram. That's why testing yourself and pushing yourself to answer questions that test higher-level thinking skills are so effective. At times, you might actually be able to feel the physical changes happening in your brain as you develop this new knowledge and these new skills. That doesn't come about without effort.

The important thing to remember is that while active revision feels much more like hard work than passive revision, you don't actually need to do nearly as much of it. That's because you remember knowledge and skills when you use active revision. When you use passive revision, it is much, much harder for the knowledge and skills to stick in your memory.

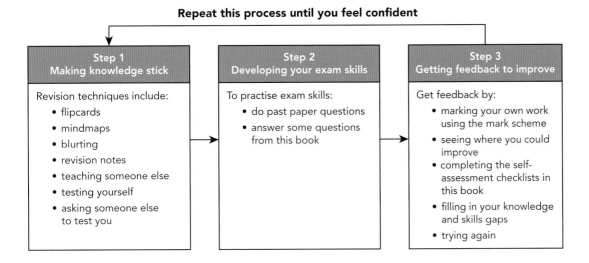

Repeat this process until you feel confident

Step 1
Making knowledge stick

Revision techniques include:
- flipcards
- mindmaps
- blurting
- revision notes
- teaching someone else
- testing yourself
- asking someone else to test you

Step 2
Developing your exam skills

To practise exam skills:
- do past paper questions
- answer some questions from this book

Step 3
Getting feedback to improve

Get feedback by:
- marking your own work using the mark scheme
- seeing where you could improve
- completing the self-assessment checklists in this book
- filling in your knowledge and skills gaps
- trying again

How to improve your exam skills

This book helps you to improve in eight different areas of exam skills, which are divided across three categories. These skills are highlighted in this book in the Exam skills focus at the start of each chapter and developed throughout the book using targeted questions, advice and reflections.

1   **Understand the questions: what are you being asked to do?**

- Know your question types.

- Understand command words.

- Work with mark scheme awareness.

2   **How to answer questions brilliantly**

- Understand connections between concepts.

- Keep to time.

- Know what a good answer looks like.

3   **Give yourself the best chance of success**

- Reflection on progress.

- How to manage test anxiety.

Understand the questions: what are you being asked to do?

Know your question types

In any exam, there will be a range of different question types. These different question types will test different types of thinking skills from Bloom's Taxonomy.

It is very important that you learn to recognise different question types. If you do lots of past papers, over time you will begin to recognise the structure of the paper for each of your subjects. You will know which types of questions may come first and which ones are more likely to come at the end of the paper. You can also complete past paper questions in the Exam practice sections in this book for additional practice.

You will also recognise the differences between questions worth a lower number of marks and questions worth more marks. The key differences are:

- how much you will need to write in your answer

- how sophisticated your answer needs to be in terms of the detail you give and the depth of thinking you show.

Types of questions

1 Multiple-choice questions

Multiple-choice questions are generally worth smaller numbers of marks. You will be given several possible answers to the question, and you will have to work out which one is correct using your knowledge and skills.

There is a chance of you getting the right answer with multiple-choice questions even if you don't know the answer. This is why you must **always give an answer for multiple-choice questions** as it means there is a chance you will earn the mark.

Multiple-choice questions are often harder than they appear. The possible answers can be very similar to each other. This means you must be confident in how you work out answers or have a high level of understanding to tell the difference between the possible answers.

Being confident in your subject knowledge and doing lots of practice multiple-choice questions will set you up for success. Use the resources in this book and the accompanying online resources to build your confidence.

This example of a multiple-choice question is worth one mark. You can see that all the answers have one part in common with at least one other answer. For example, palisade cells is included in three of the possible answers. That's why you have to really know the detail of your content knowledge to do well with multiple-choice questions.

Which two types of cells are found in plant leaves?

    A   Palisade mesophyll and stomata

    B   Palisade mesophyll and root hair

    C   Stomata and chloroplast

    D   Chloroplast and palisade mesophyll

2 Questions requiring longer-form answers

Questions requiring longer-form answers need you to write out your answer yourself.

With these questions, take careful note of how many marks are available and how much space you've been given for your answer. These two things will give you a good idea about how much you should say and how much time you should spend on the question.

A rough rule to follow is to write one sentence, or make one point, for each mark that is available. You will get better and better at these longer form questions the more you practise them.

In this example of a history question, you can see it is worth four marks. It is not asking for an explanation, just for you to list Lloyd George's aims. Therefore, you need to make four correct points in order to get full marks.

What were Lloyd George's aims during negotiations leading to the
Treaty of Versailles?   [4]

3 Essay questions

Essay questions are the longest questions you will be asked to answer in an exam. They examine the higher-order thinking skills from Bloom's Taxonomy such as analysis, synthesis and evaluation.

To do well in essay questions, you need to talk about what you know, giving your opinion, comparing one concept or example to another, and evaluating your own ideas or the ones you're discussing in your answer.

You also need to have a strong structure and logical argument that guides the reader through your thought process. This usually means having an introduction, some main body paragraphs that discuss one point at a time, and a conclusion.

Essay questions are usually level-marked. This means that you don't get one mark per point you make. Instead, you're given marks for the quality of the ideas you're sharing as well as how well you present those ideas through the subject-specific language you use and the structure of your essay.

Practising essays and becoming familiar with the mark scheme is the only way to get really good at them.

Understand command words

What are command words?

Command words are the most important words in every exam question. This is because command words tell you what you need to do in your answer. Do you remember Bloom's Taxonomy? Command words tell you which thinking skill you need to demonstrate in the answer to each question.

Two very common command words are **describe** and **explain**.

When you see the command word describe in a question, you're being asked to show lower-order thinking skills like knowledge and understanding. The question will either be worth fewer marks, or you will need to make more points if it is worth more marks.

The command word explain is asking you to show higher-order thinking skills. When you see the command word explain, you need to be able to say how or why something happens.

You need to understand all of the relevant command words for the subjects you are taking. Ask your teacher where to find them if you are not sure. It's best not to try to memorise the list of command words, but to become familiar with what command words are asking for by doing lots of practice questions and marking your own work.

How to work with command words

When you first see an exam question, read it through once. Then, read it through again and identify the command word(s). Underline the command word(s) to make it clear to yourself which they are every time you refer back to the question.

You may also want to identify the **content** words in the question and underline them with a different colour. Content words tell you which area of knowledge you need to draw on to answer the question.

In this example, command words are shown in red and content words in blue:

1   a   Explain **four** reasons why governments might support business start-ups.   [8]

   Adapted from Cambridge IGCSE Business Studies (0450)
   Q1a Paper 21 June 2022

Marking your own work using the mark scheme will help you get even better at understanding command words and knowing how to give good answers for each.

Work with mark scheme awareness

The most transformative thing that any student can do to improve their marks is to work with mark schemes. This means using mark schemes to mark your own work at every opportunity.

Many students are very nervous about marking their own work as they do not feel experienced or qualified enough. However, being brave enough to try to mark your own work and taking the time to get good at it will improve your marks hugely.

Why marking your own work makes such a big difference

Marking your own work can help you to improve your answers in the following ways:

1   **Answering the question**

   Having a deep and detailed understanding of what is required by the question enables you to answer the question more clearly and more accurately.

   It can also help you to give the required information using fewer words and in less time, as you can avoid including unrelated points or topics in your answer.

2   **Using subject-specific vocabulary**

   Every subject has subject-specific vocabulary. This includes technical terms for objects or concepts in a subject, such as mitosis and meiosis in biology. It also includes how you talk about the subject, using appropriate vocabulary that may differ from everyday language. For example, in any science subject you might be asked to describe the trend on a graph.

Your answer could say it 'goes up fast' or your answer could say it 'increases rapidly'. You would not get marks for saying 'it goes up fast', but you would for saying it 'increases rapidly'. This is the difference between everyday language and formal, scientific language.

When you answer lots of practice questions, you become fluent in the language specific to your subject.

3 Knowing how much to write

It's very common for students to either write too much or too little to answer questions. Becoming familiar with the mark schemes for many different questions will help you to gain a better understanding of how much you need to write in order to get a good mark.

4 Structuring your answer

There are often clues in questions about how to structure your answer. However, mark schemes give you an even stronger idea of the structure you should use in your answers.

For example, if a question says:

'Describe and explain two reasons why…'

You can give a clear answer by:

- Describing reason 1
- Explaining reason 1
- Describing reason 2
- Explaining reason 2

Having a very clear structure will also make it easier to identify where you have earned marks. This means that you're more likely to be awarded the number of marks you deserve.

5 Keeping to time

Answering the question, using subject-specific vocabulary, knowing how much to write and giving a clear structure to your answer will all help you to keep to time in an exam. You will not waste time by writing too much for any answer. Therefore, you will have sufficient time to give a good answer to every question.

How to answer exam questions brilliantly

Understand connections between concepts

One of the higher-level thinking skills in Bloom's Taxonomy is **synthesis**. Synthesis means making connections between different areas of knowledge. You may have heard about synoptic links. Making synoptic links is the same as showing the thinking skill of synthesis.

Exam questions that ask you to show your synthesis skills are usually worth the highest number of marks on an exam paper. To write good answers to these questions, you need to spend time thinking about the links between the topics you've studied **before** you arrive in your exam. A great way of doing this is using mind maps.

How to create a mind map

To create a mind map:

1 Use a large piece of paper and several different coloured pens.

2 Write the name of your subject in the middle. Then, write the key topic areas evenly spaced around the edge, each with a different colour.

3 Then, around each topic area, start to write the detail of what you can remember. If you find something that is connected with something you studied in another topic, you can draw a line linking the two things together.

This is a good way of practising your retrieval of information as well as linking topics together.

Answering synoptic exam questions

You will recognise questions that require you to make links between concepts because they have a higher number of marks. You will have practised them using this book and the accompanying resources.

To answer a synoptic exam question:

1 **Identify the command and content words.** You are more likely to find command words like **discuss** and **explain** in these questions. They might also have phrases like 'the connection between'.

2 **Make a plan for your answer.** It is worth taking a short amount of time to think about what you're going to write in your answer. Think carefully about what information you're going to put in, the links between the different pieces of information and how you're going to structure your answer to make your ideas clear.

3 **Use linking words and phrases in your answer.** For example, 'therefore', 'because', 'due to', 'since' or 'this means that'.

Here is an example of an English Literature exam question that requires you to make synoptic links in your answer.

1 Discuss Carol Ann Duffy's exploration of childhood in her poetry.

Refer to two poems in your answer. [25]

Content words are shown in blue; command words are shown in red.

This question is asking you to explore the theme of childhood in Duffy's poetry. You need to choose two of her poems to refer to in your answer. This means you need a good knowledge of her poetry, and to be familiar with her exploration of childhood, so that you can easily select two poems that will give you plenty to say in your answer.

Keep to time

Managing your time in exams is really important. Some students do not achieve to the best of their abilities because they run out of time to answer all the questions. However, if you manage your time well, you will be able to attempt every question on the exam paper.

Why is it important to attempt all the questions on an exam paper?

If you attempt every question on a paper, you have the best chance of achieving the highest mark you are capable of.

Students who manage their time poorly in exams will often spend far too long on some questions and not even attempt others. Most students are unlikely to get full marks on many questions, but you will get zero marks for the questions you don't answer. You can maximise your marks by giving an answer to every question.

Minutes per mark

The most important way to keep to time is knowing how many minutes you can spend on each mark.

For example, if your exam paper has 90 marks available and you have 90 minutes, you know there is 1 mark per minute.

Therefore, if you have a 5 mark question, you should spend five minutes on it.

Sometimes, you can give a good answer in less time than you have budgeted using the minutes per mark technique. If this happens, you will have more time to spend on questions that use higher-order thinking skills, or more time on checking your work.

How to get faster at answering exam questions

The best way to get faster at answering exam questions is to do lots of practice. You should practise each question type that will be in your exam, marking your own work, so that you know precisely how that question works and what is required by the question. Use the questions in this book to get better and better at answering each question type.

Use the 'Slow, Slow, Quick' technique to get faster.

Take your time answering questions when you first start practising them. You may answer them with the support of the textbook, your notes or the mark scheme. These things will support you with your content knowledge, the language you use in your answer and the structure of your answer.

Every time you practise this question type, you will get more confident and faster. You will become experienced with this question type, so that it is easy for you to recall the subject knowledge and write it down using the correct language and a good structure.

Calculating marks per minute

Use this calculation to work out how long you have for each mark:

Total time in the exam / Number of marks available = Minutes per mark

Calculate how long you have for a question worth more than one mark like this:

Minutes per mark × Marks available for this question = Number of minutes for this question

What about time to check your work?

It is a very good idea to check your work at the end of an exam. You need to work out if this is feasible with the minutes per mark available to you. If you're always rushing to finish the questions, you shouldn't budget checking time. However, if you usually have time to spare, then you can budget checking time.

To include checking time in your minutes per mark calculation:

(Total time in the exam − Checking time) / Number of marks available = Minutes per mark

---

Know what a good answer looks like

It is much easier to give a good answer if you know what a good answer looks like.

Use these methods to know what a good answer looks like.

1 **Sample answers** – you can find sample answers in these places:

   • from your teacher

   • written by your friends or other members of your class

   • in this book.

2 **Look at mark schemes** – mark schemes are full of information about what you should include in your answers. Get familiar with mark schemes to gain a better understanding of the type of things a good answer would contain.

3 **Feedback from your teacher** – if you are finding it difficult to improve your exam skills for a particular type of question, ask your teacher for detailed feedback. You should also look at their comments on your work in detail.

Give yourself the best chance of success

Reflection on progress

As you prepare for your exam, it's important to reflect on your progress. Taking time to think about what you're doing well and what could be improved brings more focus to your revision. Reflecting on progress also helps you to continuously improve your knowledge and exam skills.

How do you reflect on progress?

Use the 'reflection' feature in this book to help you reflect on your progress during your exam preparation. Then, at the end of each revision session, take a few minutes to think about the following:

	What went well? What would you do the same next time?	What didn't go well? What would you do differently next time?
Your subject knowledge		
How you revised your subject knowledge – did you use active retrieval techniques?		
Your use of subject-specific and academic language		
Understanding the question by identifying command words and content words		
Giving a clear structure to your answer		
Keeping to time		
Marking your own work		

Remember to check for silly mistakes – things like missing the units out after you carefully calculated your answer.

Use the mark scheme to mark your own work. Every time you mark your own work, you will be recognising the good and bad aspects of your work, so that you can progressively give better answers over time.

When do you need to come back to this topic or skill?

Earlier in this section of the book, we talked about revision skills and the importance of spaced retrieval. When you reflect on your progress, you need to think about how soon you need to return to the topic or skill you've just been focusing on.

For example, if you were really disappointed with your subject knowledge, it would be a good idea to do some more active retrieval and practice questions on this topic tomorrow. However, if you did really well you can feel confident you know this topic and come back to it again in three weeks' or a month's time.

The same goes for exam skills. If you were disappointed with how you answered the question, you should look at some sample answers and try this type of question again soon. However, if you did well, you can move on to other types of exam questions.

Improving your memory of subject knowledge

Sometimes students slip back into using passive revision techniques, such as only reading the coursebook or their notes, rather than also using active revision techniques, like testing themselves using flip cards or blurting.

You can avoid this mistake by observing how well your learning is working as you revise. You should be thinking to yourself, 'Am I remembering this? Am I understanding this? Is this revision working?'

If the answer to any of those questions is 'no', then you need to change what you're doing to revise this particular topic. For example, if you don't understand, you could look up your topic in a different textbook in the school library to see if a different explanation helps. Or you could see if you can find a video online that brings the idea to life.

You are in control

When you're studying for exams it's easy to think that your teachers are in charge. However, you have to remember that you are studying for your exams and the results you get will be yours and no one else's.

That means you have to take responsibility for all your exam preparation. You have the power to change how you're preparing if what you're doing isn't working. You also have control over what you revise and when: you can make sure you focus on your weaker topics and skills to improve your achievement in the subject.

This isn't always easy to do. Sometimes you have to find an inner ability that you have not used before. But, if you are determined enough to do well, you can find what it takes to focus, improve and keep going.

What is test anxiety?

Do you get worried or anxious about exams? Does your worry or anxiety impact how well you do in tests and exams?

Test anxiety is part of your natural stress response.

The stress response evolved in animals and humans many thousands of years ago to help keep them alive. Let's look at an example.

The stress response in the wild

Imagine an impala grazing in the grasslands of east Africa. It's happily and calmly eating grass in its herd in what we would call the parasympathetic state of rest and repair.

Then the impala sees a lion. The impala suddenly panics because its life is in danger. This state of panic is also known as the stressed or sympathetic state. The sympathetic state presents itself in three forms: flight, fight and freeze.

The impala starts to run away from the lion. Running away is known as the flight stress response.

The impala might not be fast enough to run away from the lion. The lion catches it but has a loose grip. The impala struggles to try to get away. This struggle is the fight stress response.

However, the lion gets an even stronger grip on the impala. Now the only chance of the impala surviving is playing dead. The impala goes limp, its heart rate and breathing slows. This is called the freeze stress response. The lion believes that it has killed the impala so it drops the impala to the ground. Now the impala can switch back into the flight response and run away.

The impala is now safe – the different stages of the stress response have saved its life.

What has the impala got to do with your exams?

When you feel test anxiety, you have the same physiological stress responses as an impala being hunted by a lion. Unfortunately, the human nervous system cannot tell the difference between a life-threatening situation, such as being chased by a lion, and the stress of taking an exam.

If you understand how the stress response works in the human nervous system, you will be able to learn techniques to reduce test anxiety.

The role of the vagus nerve in test anxiety

The vagus nerve is the part of your nervous system that determines your stress response. Vagus means 'wandering' in Latin, so the vagus nerve is also known as the 'wandering nerve'. The vagus nerve wanders from your brain, down each side of your body, to nearly all your organs, including your lungs, heart, kidneys, liver, digestive system and bladder.

If you are in a stressful situation, like an exam, your vagus nerve sends a message to all these different organs to activate their stress response. Here are some common examples:

- **Heart** beats faster.

- **Kidneys** produce more adrenaline so that you can run, making you fidgety and distracted.

- **Digestive system** and **bladder** want to eliminate all waste products so that energy can be used for fight or flight.

If you want to feel calmer about your revision and exams, you need to do two things to help you move into the parasympathetic, or rest and repair, state:

1   Work with your vagus nerve to send messages of safety through your body.

2   Change your perception of the test so that you see it as safe and not dangerous.

How to cope with test anxiety

1   Be well prepared

Good preparation is the most important part of managing test anxiety. The better your preparation, the more confident you will be. If you are confident, you will not perceive the test or exam as dangerous, so the sympathetic nervous system responses of fight, flight and freeze are less likely to happen.

This book is all about helping you to be well prepared and building your confidence in your knowledge and ability to answer exam questions well. Working through the knowledge recall questions will help you to become more confident in your knowledge of the subject. The practice questions and exam skills questions will help you to become more confident in communicating your knowledge in an exam.

To be well prepared, look at the advice in the rest of this chapter and use it as you work through the questions in this book.

2   Work with your vagus nerve

The easiest way to work with your vagus nerve to tell it that you're in a safe situation is through your breathing. This means breathing deeply into the bottom of your lungs, so that your stomach expands, and then breathing out for longer than you breathed in. You can do this with counting.

Breathe in deeply, expanding your abdomen, for the count of four; breathe out drawing your navel back towards your spine for the count of five, six or seven. Repeat this at least three times. However, you can do it for as long as it takes for you to feel calm.

The important thing is that you breathe out for longer than you breathe in. This is because when you breathe in, your heart rate increases slightly, and when you breathe out, your heart rate decreases slightly. If you're spending more time breathing out overall, you will be decreasing your heart rate over time.

3   Feel it

Anxiety is an uncomfortable, difficult thing to feel. That means that many people try to run away from anxious feelings. However, this means the stress just gets stored in your body for you to feel later.

When you feel anxious, follow these four steps:

1   Pause.

2   Place one hand on your heart and one hand on your stomach.

3   Notice what you're feeling.

4   Stay with your feelings.

What you will find is that if you are willing to experience what you feel for a minute or two, the feeling of anxiety will usually pass very quickly.

4 Write or talk it out

If your thoughts are moving very quickly, it is often better to get them out of your mind and on to paper.

You could take a few minutes to write down everything that comes through your mind, then rip up your paper and throw it away. If you don't like writing, you can speak aloud alone or to someone you trust.

Other ways to break the stress cycle

Exercise and movement	Being friendly	Laughter
• Run or walk. • Dance. • Lift weights. • Yoga. Anything that involves moving your body is helpful.	• Chat to someone in your study break. • Talk to the cashier when you buy your lunch.	• Watch or listen to a funny show on TV or online. • Talk with someone who makes you laugh. • Look at photos of fun times.
Have a hug	Releasing emotions	Creativity
• Hug a friend or relative. • Cuddle a pet e.g. a cat. Hug for 20 seconds or until you feel calm and relaxed.	It is healthy to release negative or sad emotions. Crying is often a quick way to get rid of these difficult feelings so if you feel like you need to cry, allow it.	• Paint, draw or sketch. • Sew, knit or crochet. • Cook, build something.

If you have long-term symptoms of anxiety, it is important to tell someone you trust and ask for help.

Your perfect revision session

1 Intention

What do you want to achieve in this revision session?
- Choose an area of knowledge or an exam skill that you want to focus on.
- Choose some questions from this book that focus on this knowledge area or skill.
- Gather any other resources you will need e.g. pen, paper, flashcards, coursebook.

2 Focus

Set your focus for the session
- Remove distractions from your study area e.g. leave your phone in another room.
- Write down on a piece of paper or sticky note the knowledge area or skill you're intending to focus on.
- Close your eyes and take three deep breaths, with the exhale longer than the inhale.

3 Revision

Revise your knowledge and understanding
- To improve your knowledge and understanding of the topic, use your coursebook, notes or flashcards, including active learning techniques.
- To improve your exam skills, look at previous answers, teacher feedback, mark schemes, sample answers or examiners' reports.

4 Practice

Answer practice questions
- Use the questions in this book, or in the additional online resources, to practise your exam skills.
- If the exam is soon, do this in timed conditions without the support of the coursebook or your notes.
- If the exam is a long time away, you can use your notes and resources to help you.

5 Feedback

Mark your answers
- Use mark schemes to mark your work.
- Reflect on what you've done well and what you could do to improve next time.

6 Next steps

What have you learned about your progress from this revision session? What do you need to do next?
- What did you do well? Feel good about these things, and know it's safe to set these things aside for a while.
- What do you need to work on? How are you going to improve? Make a plan to get better at the things you didn't do well or didn't know.

7 Rest

Take a break
- Do something completely different to rest: get up, move or do something creative or practical.
- Remember that rest is an important part of studying, as it gives your brain a chance to integrate your learning.

1 Characteristics and classification of living organisms

An important part of understanding exam questions is to know what command words are and what they mean. Command words are specific instructions in questions that help you to plan and structure your answer. In this chapter you will practise your understanding of the command word 'explain'.

It is important that you understand what this command word is instructing you to do.

Explain	set out purposes or reasons/make the relationships between things evident/provide why and/or how and support with relevant evidence.

Explanation questions usually need a longer response and are usually worth between 2 and 6 marks.

When asked to provide an explanation, you should aim to give reasons for the data, or phenomenon, you are provided with. Be sure to include as much evidence, from the question or from your own knowledge, to strengthen your response. Make sure you plan your answer to cover all the points you need to include in your answer.

1.1 Characteristics of living organisms

1 Living organisms share many characteristics. Think about three organisms of your choice and answer the following questions.

  a What is one thing that your three organisms have in common?

  b What is one unique thing that each organism is able to do?

2 Consider the list of key terms below.

> photosynthesis   movement   growth   feeding   respiration

  a Name the characteristics that are common to both plants and animals.   [1]

  b Identify the characteristic(s) that are common to plants only.   [1]

  c A student investigated the behaviour of earthworms in response to light. At the start of the experiment, the equipment was set up as in Figure 1.1. After 10 minutes, the earthworms were found to be in the covered part of the tray.

UNDERSTAND THESE TERMS
• movement
• respiration
• sensitivity
• growth
• reproduction
• excretion
• nutrition

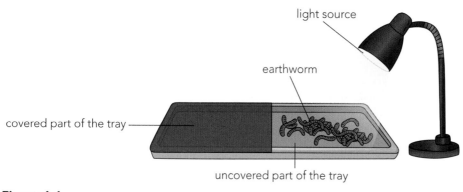

light source

earthworm

covered part of the tray

uncovered part of the tray

Figure 1.1

  Describe and explain which characteristics of life were demonstrated in this investigation.   [3]

  [Total: 5]

REFLECTION

A mnemonic is a short word or statement that can be used to remember a larger amount of information. For example, the first letters of a series of words in a sentence can be the same as the first letters in a list. Think of a mnemonic to help you recall the seven characteristics of living organisms. When you have done this, consider how you can better remember which key terms are associated with each of these seven characteristics. How could you better link these terms with their appropriate characteristics?

1.2 The biological classification system

1   What are the similarities between you, a chimpanzee and a eucalyptus tree?

2   Figure 1.2 shows five animals. Their binomial names are provided.

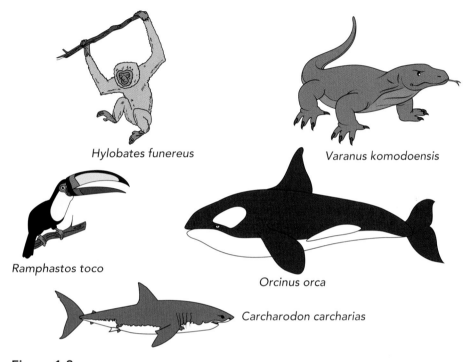

Hylobates funereus

Varanus komodoensis

Ramphastos toco

Orcinus orca

Carcharodon carcharias

Figure 1.2

a   Describe what is meant by the binominal system of naming species.   [2]
b   List three genera shown in Figure 1.2.   [3]
c   State which two animals are more closely related to each other
than the others.   [1]

[Total: 6]

UNDERSTAND THESE TERMS
• binomial
• genus
• species

3   Suggest why your answer to **2c** would be supported by evidence
obtained from the base sequence of DNA.   **[Total: 1]**

4   Using examples from this chapter, what is meant by the term 'species'?

« RECALL AND CONNECT 1 «

The three species of elephant are the African bush elephant, African forest elephant and the Asian elephant. These are *Loxodonta africana*, *Loxodonta cyclotis* and *Elephas maximus* respectively.

State two advantages of using the internationally agreed binomial naming system rather than the common naming system to identify elephants.

REFLECTION

What are the rules you should remember when you write down the binomial name of an organism? How can you help yourself to avoid forgetting them?

1.3 Keys

1   Think of some objects in your home or school that require being organised in some way, such as cutlery in a drawer or items of laboratory equipment. On what basis are these objects separated from one another?

2   Keys used in biological identification are usually dichotomous.

    a   State what is meant by the term 'dichotomous'. [1]

    b   Construct a dichotomous key to classify each of the five animals in Figure 1.2. [5]

                                                      [Total: 6]

UNDERSTAND THESE TERMS
• characteristic
• dichotomous
• key

3   Construct a dichotomous key to show how humans can be separated from two other animals.

1.4 Kingdoms

1   Make a list of the first 10–20 organisms that you think of. How many of them are animals? How many of them are plants? How many of them are neither animals nor plants?

2   Living organisms can be grouped into five kingdoms.

    a   State one difference between organisms in the animal and plant kingdoms. [1]

    b   Some protoctists, prokaryotes and fungi are unicellular (consist of only one cell). State a characteristic that can be used to classify unicellular organisms into these kingdoms. [1]

                                                      [Total: 2]

3 All living organisms can be classified based on shared features.

    a Plants and fungi are two kingdoms into which some living organisms can be placed. Name the other three. [1]

    b For a long time, fungi were classified as plants. Describe one of the features that differ between living organisms in the plant and fungi kingdoms that helped to reclassify them. [1]

[Total: 2]

> **UNDERSTAND THESE TERMS**
> - kingdom
> - protoctist
> - prokaryote
> - fungus

4 Draw a table to summarise the distinguishing features of organisms that belong to each of the five kingdoms.

1.5 Groups within the animal and plant kingdoms

1 Are humans more closely related to spiders or to fish? Explain your answer.

2 Copy and complete the following sentences by filling in missing words:

There are five .... of organisms. Two of these are the animals and plants.

Animals can be arranged into several groups, including vertebrates and arthropods.

Vertebrates all have a .... However, there are five different groups of vertebrate: ...., ..., ..., ... and .... Another group are the arthropods. These can be further subdivided into more groups, including the ...., which have four pairs of legs and ...., which have three pairs of legs.

Plants are either ferns or flowering plants. Ferns produce .... to reproduce. Flowering plants can be subdivided into groups called .... and .... These differ based on several characteristics, including the shape of organs such as the .... and ....

> **UNDERSTAND THESE TERMS**
> - arthropod
> - fern
> - flowering plant
> - vertebrate

3 Figure 1.3 shows the five types of vertebrates, arranged into two groups in a simple dichotomous key.

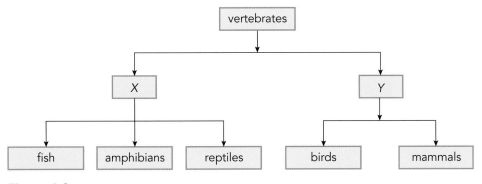

Figure 1.3

a   Identify a feature that all vertebrates have in common.   [1]

b   Give two features of reptiles that distinguish them from amphibians
    and fish.   [2]

c   Give two features of mammals that distinguish them from birds.   [2]

d   Suggest the features of *X* and *Y* that were used to distinguish the
    two groups of vertebrates.   [1]

[Total: 6]

≪ RECALL AND CONNECT 2 ≪

List the unique features of these two groups of organism: vertebrates
and arthropods.

REFLECTION

Try to explain what is meant by the term 'kingdom' when referring to
classification of organisms. What could you do to help you explain this
concept better?

Supplement: how can you better remember the features of the five kingdoms
of organisms?

> 1.6 Viruses

1   List the seven characteristics of life.

2   Suggest why viruses are not considered to be living organisms.   **[Total: 2]**

3   Order the following structures in terms of size: human cell, virus,
    bacterium (prokaryote).

UNDERSTAND THESE TERMS
• virus
• genetic material
• protein coat

REFLECTION

There is one question in this chapter that includes both the 'describe' *and*
'explain' command words and this is quite common in exam questions. Make
sure you include *both* the description and the explanation in your answers to
these questions. How confident do you feel that you understand the command
words 'describe' and 'explain' and the difference between them?

SELF-ASSESSMENT CHECKLIST

Let's revisit the Knowledge focus and Exam skills focus for this chapter.

Decide how confident you are with each statement.

Now I can:	Show it	Needs more work	Almost there	Confident to move on
outline the seven characteristics of living organisms	Write down the seven characteristics of living organisms and then make each term the centre of a mind map that shows key terms associated with each.			
explain how the binomial system is used to name organisms	Write a sentence including the words 'genus' and 'species'.			
use and construct keys	Construct a dichotomous key that enables you to group different items of laboratory equipment.			
describe how to classify vertebrates and arthropods	Draw a table to show the key features of vertebrates and arthropods.			
describe the features of the five kingdoms of organisms	Write a series of multiple-choice questions that consider the features of the five kingdoms of organisms (with correct answers) to test a classmate.			
describe how to classify ferns and flowering plants	Draw a Venn diagram to show the similarities and differences between ferns and flowering plants.			
outline the features of viruses	Draw a diagram that shows the simplified structure of a virus.			
understand the 'explain' command word.	Write a question about characteristics and classification that includes the command word 'explain'.			

2 Cells

Biology exam questions will often come with images, diagrams, tables or graphs. You need to be able to use these to your advantage in the exams. They can be just for guidance (for example, a picture of a species of plant or animal that you may not be familiar with) but often they contain information that will help you answer the question. As you go through this chapter, as well as the rest of the book, you will come across numerous images, graphs and tables. Consider how to best use them in your answers.

You will come across questions using the 'calculate' command word in this topic.

Calculate	work out from given facts, figures or information.

You must remember to show all the steps in your working when answering 'calculate' questions. This is because you may receive marks for using the correct method, even if you have used the wrong values in your answer. You should also include the correct units in your answer: remember not to confuse millimetres with microns!

A good answer to 'calculate' questions includes:

- showing the mathematical steps you took leading to the answer
- using appropriate units
- using an appropriate number of significant figures asked for in the question.

2.1 Animal and plants cells

1   **a**   Write down six components of a typical animal cell.

      b   Write down eight components of a typical plant cell.

      c   How can you identify whether a cell is a plant cell or an animal cell?

      d   Write down the function of each of the components listed in **a** and **b**.

2   Figure 2.1 is a micrograph of an unknown tissue.

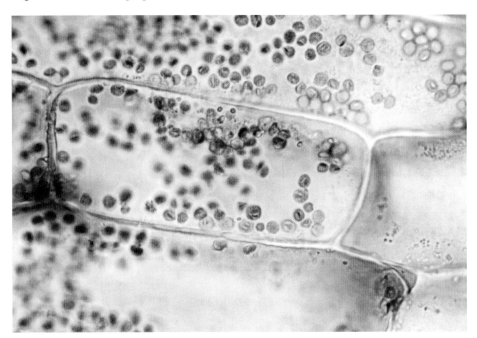

Figure 2.1: Micrograph of an unknown tissue

  a   State whether the tissue in Figure 2.1 is an animal or a plant tissue.   [1]

  b   Explain, using two visible components, why this is the case.   [2]

  c   Describe the function of the two components identified in **b**.   [2]

d　Figure 2.2 shows a diagram of an animal cell.

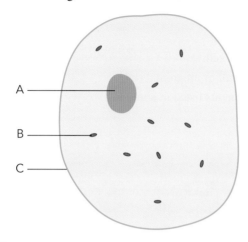

Figure 2.2

Using Figure 2.2, copy and complete the following table:

Function	Name	Label
The site where the genetic material is stored.		
	mitochondrion	
A partially permeable barrier separating the cell from the outside environment.		

[3]

[Total: 8]

≪ RECALL AND CONNECT 1 ≪

Look back at Chapter 1: Characteristics and classification of living organisms. Name the differences between organisms in the animal and plant kingdoms.

UNDERSTAND THESE TERMS

- partially permeable
- mitochondrion
- ribosomes

2.2 Bacterial cells

1   Bacterial cells are always exposed to their environment as they are unicellular.

   a   What is the bacterial cell wall made from?

   b   What part of the cell controls the movement of substances into and out of the cell?

2   a   What parts of the bacterial cell are also found in animal and plant cells?

   b   Draw a table comparing the structure of bacterial, plant and animal cells.

3   Figure 2.3 is a diagram of a typical prokaryotic cell.

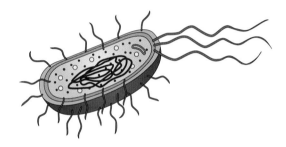

Figure 2.3

   a   State three differences between the cell in Figure 2.3 and a typical animal cell.   [3]

   b   Define the term 'plasmid'.   [1]

[Total: 4]

> **UNDERSTAND THESE TERMS**
> * bacteria
> * prokaryotic cells
> * plasmid

REFLECTION

The identification of the three main types of cells is included in questions that will appear often in assessments. How can you improve your memory of these cells and their features? Try drawing and labelling them or making comparative tables. Be sure to include similarities as well as differences!

2.3 Specialised cells

1 **a** Why can only multicellular organisms have specialised cells?

   b Make a list of four specialised cell types (two each from animals and plants). State their functions and where in the organism they are found.

2 **a** What is the best way to describe the relationship between the terms cell, tissue, organ and organ system?

   b Specialised cells have adaptations that allow them to carry out their functions. State which cellular components will be present in high numbers in a muscle cell but present in low numbers in a fat cell.

3 Copy and complete the following table using appropriate terms.

Specialised cell type	Function
	transport oxygen
palisade mesophyll cell	
	male gamete in animal reproduction
	absorption of water and minerals in plants
neurone	

[Total: 5]

UNDERSTAND THESE TERMS
• tissue
• organ
• organ system

2.4 Sizes of specimens

1 Write down all three possible versions of the magnification equation that can be used to work out magnification, image size and actual size.

2 **a** How many μm are in 3.4 mm?

   b How many metres are 4.2×10^6 μm?

3 Figure 2.4 shows an electron micrograph of a tardigrade.
This tardigrade is 0.5 mm long. Calculate the magnification of the image. **[Total: 2]**

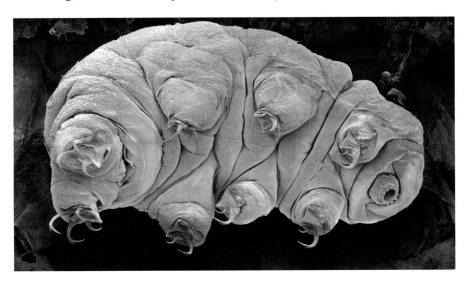

Figure 2.4: A tardigrade

4 Figure 2.5 is a cross-section of a leaf. The actual size of the cross-section
of this leaf is 235 μm. Calculate the magnification of the image. **[Total: 3]**

UNDERSTAND THIS TERM
• magnification

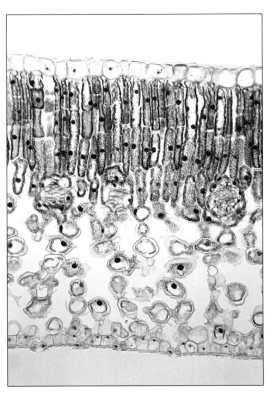

Figure 2.5

SELF-ASSESSMENT CHECKLIST

Let's revisit the Knowledge focus and Exam skills focus for this chapter.

Decide how confident you are with each statement.

Now I can:	Show it	Needs more work	Almost there	Confident to move on
find out about the structure of the cells of animals, plants and bacteria	Make a table comparing the structure of animal, plant and bacterial cells.			
recall the functions of each of the parts of these cells	State the function of all eight components of a typical plant cell.			
describe how the structures of some specialised cells are adapted to their functions	Name three specialised cells and describe how their structure allows them to carry out a named function.			
practise using the magnification equation	Find micrographs online and calculate their magnification until you are fluent.			
understand the command word 'calculate' and answer a 'calculate' question	Compare your answers to the 'calculate' questions in this chapter to those provided and make a list of any information that you missed.			
understand how to answer questions that contain diagrams.	Compare your answers to the questions containing diagrams in this chapter to those provided and make a list of any information that you missed.			

3 Movement into and out of cells

The 'state' command word is often used for short-answer questions. You will be expected to provide a fact or short answer in your response.

State	express in clear terms.

You are not expected to provide detailed explanations or descriptions for this command word. It is often combined with another word, such as 'explain' or 'suggest'. When you come across questions with two command words make sure you include answers to both command words in your answer.

3.1 Diffusion

1   Consider a human cell and a plant cell.

    a   Which structure affects whether a substance can move into both cells?

    b   Why would this process take more time with the plant cell than the human cell?

2   Diffusion is a process by which substances move into and out of cells.

    a   Explain the role of the particles' kinetic energy during the process
of diffusion.   [2]

    b   Give one reason why diffusion of gases is important for organisms.   [1]

    c   A student listed some factors that can be changed in laboratory
investigations.

> temperature   pH   surface area   distance
> concentration gradient   mass of particles

    i   State which factor is least likely to influence the rate of diffusion.   [1]

    ii   Choose one of the other factors listed by the student. Explain
how this factor affects the rate of diffusion.   [2]

[Total: 6]

3   Why is the term 'net' important when defining the term 'osmosis'?

≪ RECALL AND CONNECT 1 ≪

Look back at Chapter 2: Cells. List the molecules that are often absorbed
by animal cells and the molecules that are often excreted by those cells.
How do these differ from those absorbed and excreted by green plant cells?

UNDERSTAND THESE TERMS

- concentration gradient
- diffusion
- kinetic energy
- net movement
- random
- surface area

3.2 Osmosis

1   Define the term 'diffusion'.

2   State the name of the cell structure that water diffuses through.   **[Total: 1]**

3   Copy and complete the following sentences using appropriate terms:

Osmosis is the .... movement of water molecules from a region
of .... water .... (dilute solution) to a region of
.... water .... (concentrated solution), through
a .... permeable membrane.   **[Total: 6]**

4 Figure 3.1 shows an investigation into the effect of water potential and temperature on the mass of a piece of plant tissue. The tissues from carrot P and carrot Q are submerged in two solutions of different concentration.

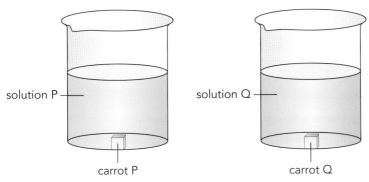

Figure 3.1: The equipment used in an investigation into the effect of water potential and temperature on the mass of a piece of plant tissue

a Explain why the two pieces of carrot must have the same mass and water potential. [1]

b Suggest why the carrot used in this investigation must be fresh, rather than boiled. [2]

c Figure 3.2 shows the results of this investigation.

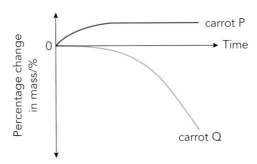

Figure 3.2

i The solution containing carrot P was kept at a constant temperature, but the temperature of the solution containing carrot Q was increased. Explain how Figure 3.2 shows this. [2]

iii State which solution had the highest water potential. Explain your answer. [3]

iii Draw diagrams to compare the appearance of a plant cell extracted from the tissues in carrot P and carrot Q at the end of this investigation. [2]

iv Explain why this investigation could not be undertaken with animal tissue. [2]

[Total: 12]

UNDERSTAND THESE TERMS

- flaccid
- partially permeable membrane
- solvent
- turgid
- water potential

5   Outline how an investigation using a partially permeable membrane, such as dialysis tubing, could be used to investigate the process of osmosis. You may draw a simple diagram in your response.

≪ RECALL AND CONNECT 2 ≪

What part of an animal cell contains the most water? What additional structure in plant cells also contains a lot of water?

3.3 Active transport

1   Why is a concentration gradient required for diffusion to occur?

2   Define the term 'active transport'.   **[Total: 2]**

3   Figure 3.3 shows how the rate of entry of a substance X by active transport changes as the concentration of substance X changes outside the cell.

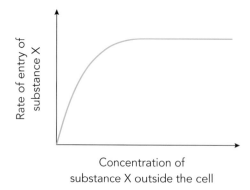

Figure 3.3

a   Describe the shape of the graph shown in Figure 3.3.   [1]

b   Explain how the shape of the graph shown in Figure 3.3 is determined by the requirement of protein carriers in active transport.   [1]

c   Explain why root hair cells must use active transport, rather than diffusion, to absorb mineral ions from the soil.   [1]

[Total: 3]

≪ RECALL AND CONNECT 3 ≪

Which characteristic of living organisms is required to release energy?

REFLECTION

How will you remember the similarities and differences between diffusion, active transport and osmosis? One technique is to use a Venn diagram – can you think of any others?

UNDERSTAND THESE TERMS

- energy
- protein carriers
- root hairs

SELF-ASSESSMENT CHECKLIST

Let's revisit the Knowledge focus and Exam skills focus for this chapter.

Decide how confident you are with each statement.

Now I can:	Show it	Needs more work	Almost there	Confident to move on
outline the process of diffusion and its importance to organisms	Write down the definition of the term 'diffusion'.			
explain how some factors affect the rate of diffusion	Write a sentence including the terms 'temperature', 'kinetic energy' and 'rate of diffusion'.			
understand that osmosis is a special kind of diffusion, involving water	Explain how osmosis differs from diffusion.			
describe how to investigate osmosis, using dialysis tubing and plant tissues	Draw diagrams to show how an investigation can be undertaken to investigate osmosis using dialysis tubing and plant tissues.			

CONTINUED

Now I can:	Show it	Needs more work	Almost there	Confident to move on
describe the process of active transport	Write a series of multiple-choice questions (with correct answers) to test a classmate about the process of active transport.			
describe what is meant by the term 'water potential'	Draw Venn diagrams to show the similarities and differences between the effects of solutions with a very low and a very high water potential on human and plant cells.			
explain how osmosis affects plant cells	Draw a table to show the similarities and differences between the effect of solutions with different water potentials on the structure of plant cells.			
explain how active transport happens	List the factors required for active transport that are not required for diffusion.			
understand the command word 'state' and answer a 'state' question.	Pick an Exam skill question in this chapter that uses the command word 'state' and compare your answer to the answers supplied.			

Exam practice 1

This section contains past paper questions from previous Cambridge exams, which draw together your knowledge on a range of topics that you have covered up to this point. These questions give you the opportunity to test your knowledge and understanding. Additional past paper practice questions can be found in the accompanying digital material.

The following question has an example student response and commentary provided. Once you have worked through the question, read the student response and commentary. Are your answers different to the example response?

1   Fig 1.1 shows five species of mollusc.

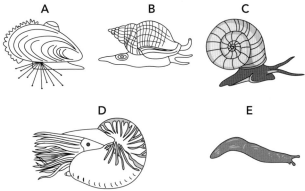

Fig 1.1

a   Use the key to identify each species. Write the letter of each species (**A** to **E**) in the correct box beside the key. [3]

Key

1	**a**	body is completely or partly covered in a shell	go to 2	
	b	body is not completely covered or partly covered in a shell	*Limax flavus*	
2	**a**	shell is attached to rocks by thin threads	*Mytilus edulis*	
	b	shell is not attached to rocks by thin threads	go to 3	
3	**a**	shell is a spire that comes to a point	*Buccinum undatum*	
	b	shell is not a spire that comes to a point	go to 4	
4	**a**	animal has tentacles	*Nautilus pompilius*	
	b	animal has 2 tentacles	*Planorbis planorbis*	

b   State **two** features that are shown by all molluscs. [2]

[Total: 5]

Cambridge IGCSE Biology (0610) Paper 31 Q1, June 2015

Example student response						Commentary
1 **a**	**1 a**	body is completely or partly covered in a shell	go to 2			This response correctly identifies the first three species, listed as E, A and B. However, the fourth and fifth species are in the wrong order, so one of the three available marks is withheld. *This answer is awarded 2 out of 3 marks.*
	b	body is not completely covered or partly covered in a shell	*Limax flavus*	E		
	2 a	shell is attached to rocks by thin threads	*Mytilus edulis*	A		
	b	shell is not attached to rocks by thin threads	go to 3			
	3 a	shell is a spire that comes to a point	*Buccinum undatum*	B		
	b	shell is not a spire that comes to a point	go to 4			
	4 a	animal has tentacles	*Nautilus pompilius*	C		
	b	animal has two tentacles	*Planorbis planorbis*	D		
b	They have segments. They have a slimy body, covered in mucus.					The student's first statement is incorrect: molluscs do not have segments. They are unsegmented organisms. However, a mark can be awarded for their second point, as molluscs do have a slimy body. *This answer is awarded 1 out of 2 marks.*

Now you have read the commentary to the previous question, here is a similar question that you should attempt. Use the information from the previous response and commentary to guide you.

2 All living organisms are placed into groups according to their features.

Myriapods are one of the main groups of arthropods.

a State **two** features of myriapods that can be used to distinguish them from other arthropods. [2]

Fig 2.1 shows that there are four main groups of arthropods.

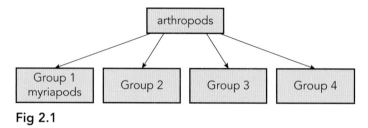

Fig 2.1

b State the names of **two** of the other groups of arthropods in Fig 2.1.   [2]

[Total: 4]

Cambridge IGCSE Biology (0610) Paper 41 Q1a, b, November 2019

The following question has an example student commentary and answer provided. Work through the question first, then compare your answer to the sample answer and commentary. Are your answers different to the sample response? Identify how you could improve your answer.

3 Many organisms have adaptations that increase the area of their gas exchange surfaces.

Fig 3.1 is a photomicrograph of part of a fish gill.

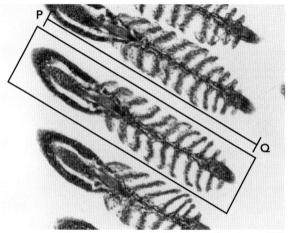

magnification x 550

Fig 3.1

Measure the length of line **PQ** in Fig 3.1.

length of line **PQ** .... mm

Calculate the actual length of the part of the fish gill using the formula and your measurement.

magnification = length of line **PQ**/actual length of the part of the fish gill

Give your answer to **three** decimal places.

[Total: 3]

Cambridge IGCSE Biology (0610) Paper 62 Q1c ii, March 2022

Example student response	Commentary
Length of line = 5.4 mm. Magnification = 5.4/actual length. Actual length = 5.4/550 = 0.00981 mm.	The measurement of line PQ is too short. The student has measured in centimetres rather than millimetres.
	The student did rearrange the formula and calculated the value correctly allowing for the error carried forward in the measurement. However, they have written their answer down to five decimal points, confusing significant figures with decimal points. *This answer is awarded 1 out of 3 marks.*

The following question has an example student commentary and answer provided. Work through the question first, then compare your answer to the sample answer and commentary. Do you feel you need to improve your understanding of this topic?

4 A biologist made a slide of some epidermal cells from a scale leaf of an onion bulb. Fig 4.1 is a drawing that the biologist made of one of the cells.

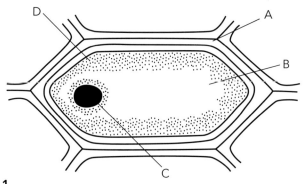

Fig 4.1

a Table 4.1 shows the functions of the structures within a plant cell.

Complete Table 4.1 by:

- naming the part of the cell that carries out each function
- using the letters from Fig 4.1 to identify the part of the cell named.

function	letter from Fig 4.1	name
resists the turgor pressure of the cell		
controls the activities of the cell		
site of the chemical reactions of the cell including synthesis of proteins		

Table 4.1

[3]

b The biologist added a few drops of concentrated salt solution to the cells on the slide and took a photograph of the cells, as shown in Fig 4.2.

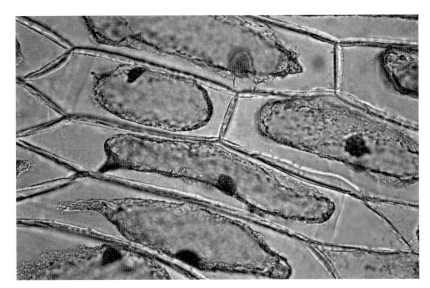

Fig 4.2

    i With reference to Fig 4.2, describe the effect on the plant cells of adding a concentrated salt solution. [3]

    ii Use the term **water potential** to explain the effect you have described. [3]

[Total: 9]

Adapted from Cambridge IGCSE Biology (0610) Paper 31 Q4, June 2015

Example student response				Commentary
4 **a**	function	letter from Fig 4.1	name	This response correctly identifies the parts of the cell labelled C and D as the nucleus and ribosome. However, the student incorrectly identifies the vacuole as the structure that resists the turgor pressure of the cell. *This answer is awarded 2 out of 3 marks.*
	resists the turgor pressure of the cell	B	*vacuole*	
	controls the activities of the cell	C	*nucleus*	
	site of the chemical reactions of the cell including synthesis of proteins	D	*ribosome*	
b **i**	*The cell's cytoplasm and vacuole has become smaller. The cell membrane has pulled away from the cell wall.*			The student gains credit for identifying the reduction in the volume of the cytoplasm and vacuole and correctly describes the effect on the cell membrane. The third mark is not awarded because the state of the cell is not given. *This answer is awarded 2 out of 3 marks.*

Example student response	Commentary
ii The salt solution has a lower concentration of water than the cell, so water moves out of cells by osmosis through the cell membrane.	Here, the student incorrectly uses the term 'water concentration' and does not mention the important feature of the cell membrane. However, one mark can still be awarded, for the mention of osmosis being responsible for water molecules moving out of the cell. *This answer is awarded 1 out of 3 marks.*

4 Biological molecules

KNOWLEDGE FOCUS

In this chapter you will answer questions on:

* carbohydrates, fats and proteins

 the structure of DNA.

EXAM SKILLS FOCUS

In this chapter you will:

* show that you understand the difference between the 'describe' and 'state' command words.

A 'state' command usually word requires you to give a simple answer, or a single chemical formula or an equation. 'Describe' questions require you to give an account of whatever is asked for in the question. 'Describe' can also be used in questions where you are asked to analyse a graph or a data set. In this chapter you will practise your understanding of the command words 'describe' and 'state', the difference between them and how answers to each of these types of question should be presented.

It is important that you understand what each command word is instructing you to do.

Describe	state the points of a topic or give characteristics and main features.
State	express in clear terms.

4.1 Carbohydrates, fats and proteins

1   This question is about carbohydrates.

    a   Which chemical elements make up carbohydrates?

    b   Describe how you would test a particular food item for starch and reducing sugars.

2   This question is about lipids and proteins.

    a   What is the main difference between the structure of a carbohydrate and a lipid?

    b   Which element is found in proteins but is not found in carbohydrates and lipids?

    c   Describe how you would test a particular food for protein and lipids.

3   Carbohydrates are one of the main groups of biological molecules.

    a   Describe the structure of a cellulose molecule.   [2]

    b   Explain how the test for reducing sugars could be used to compare the glucose content of two different breakfast cereals.   [3]

[Total: 5]

> UNDERSTAND THESE TERMS
> * carbohydrates
> * Benedict's solution

> UNDERSTAND THESE TERMS
> * lipids
> * emulsion
> * protein

4   Copy and complete the following table:

Reagent name	Positive test result	Tests for this group of biological molecules
iodine solution		
		reducing sugars
	a white, cloudy emulsion is formed	
		proteins

[Total: 4]

5   Proteins come in many shapes and sizes, but they are all made from the
     same elements.

   a   State the four elements that are found in all proteins.   [2]

   b   Figure 4.1 shows the structure of two different proteins **a** haemoglobin
     and **b** keratin. Explain why different proteins have different structures.   [3]

[Total: 5]

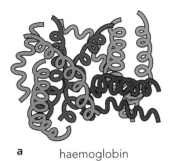 

   a   haemoglobin   **b**   keratin

Figure 4.1

REFLECTION

Questions 3a and 5a contain the 'describe' and 'state' command words – how
well do you feel you answered these questions? What could you do to ensure
you fully understand what these command words mean and what is required in
answers to such questions?

4.2 The structure of DNA

《 RECALL AND CONNECT 1 《

Look back at Chapter 2: Cells. Where is DNA is stored in the cell?

1   a   What is the function of DNA?

   b   How can you use the DNA sequence of the first strand of a DNA molecule
     to work out the DNA sequence of a second strand of the same DNA
     molecule?

2   Figure 4.2 shows the structure of DNA.

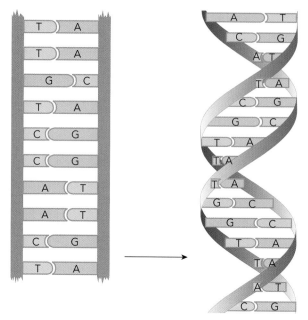

Figure 4.2: The structure of DNA

a   Describe the structure of DNA.   [4]

b   20% of the bases in a section of DNA are A. Describe a method
     to calculate the proportion of the G base in the DNA strand.   [3]

[Total: 7]

SELF-ASSESSMENT CHECKLIST

Let's revisit the Knowledge focus and Exam skills focus for this chapter.

Decide how confident you are with each statement.

Now I can:	Show it	Needs more work	Almost there	Confident to move on
find out about the components of carbohydrates, proteins and lipids	Describe the differences between carbohydrates, proteins and lipids.			
use food tests to detect the presence of different biological molecules	State how to test food for: a proteins b reducing sugars.			
outline the structure of DNA	State the function of DNA.			
understand the difference between the 'describe' and 'state' command words.	Write two 'describe' and two 'state' questions using the material covered in this chapter and provide answers.			

5 Enzymes

Questions that feature the command words 'predict' and 'explain' are among the most challenging to answer. When asked to make a prediction, you are expected to suggest what may happen based on available evidence. To do this successfully, it is important that you use all the information you have been provided with in your answer. You may also be expected to include your own knowledge of the topic when making predictions. When asked to provide an explanation, give reasons for the data, or phenomenon, you are provided with. Be sure to state as much evidence from the question, or from your own knowledge, to strengthen your response. Look out for the question that contains both of these command words in this chapter and make sure your response covers what is required for each.

Predict	suggest what may happen based on available information.
Explain	set out purposes or reasons/make the relationships between things evident/provide why and/or how and support with relevant evidence.

5.1 Biological catalysts

1   Enzymes are biological catalysts that increase the rate of chemical reactions
    in all living organisms.

    a   What type of biological molecule are enzymes?

    b   What is an example of a chemical reaction that happens in all living organisms?

2   Lipase is an enzyme that digests lipids into fatty acids and glycerol in the
    small intestine.

    a   State what is meant by the term 'enzyme'.   [2]

    b   Orlistat is a drug that some people take to lose weight. Figure 5.1
        shows molecules of orlistat, a lipid and lipase.

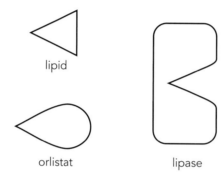

lipid

orlistat   lipase

Figure 5.1

Using this information, suggest how orlistat could help some people
to lose weight.   [4]

[Total: 6]

3   Using a diagram, describe how the shape of an enzyme is important for
    its function.

4   Explain the action of enzymes.   **[Total: 4]**

≪ RECALL AND CONNECT 1 ≪

Look back at Chapter 4: Biological molecules. Most enzymes are proteins.
How could you test for the presence of an enzyme in a solution?

UNDERSTAND THESE TERMS

- catalyst
- enzyme
- substrate
- chemical reaction

REFLECTION

How confident are you that you could explain what is meant by the term
'complementary' when referring to the way in which enzymes work?
What could you do to help you explain this concept better?

5.2 Factors that affect enzymes

1 State the optimum temperature and pH for human amylase.

2 A Petri dish was filled with agar mixed with albumin, a protein found in egg.
Four holes were cut in the milk agar and each hole was filled with one substance
(Figure 5.2). Well P contains protease in the presence of a strong acid. Well Q
contains protease that has been previously boiled. Well R contains protease
in the presence of a strong alkali. Well S contains distilled water.

After incubating the plate at room temperature for 24 hours, biuret solution
was added to the whole dish.

UNDERSTAND THESE TERMS
• complementary
• denaturation
• kinetic energy
• optimum

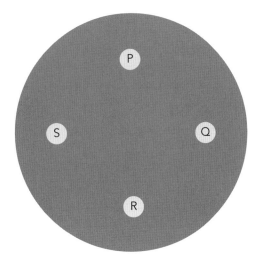

Figure 5.2

a Describe how protease affects the albumin protein.   [1]
b Predict and explain the results of this investigation for wells P, Q and R.   [4]
c Explain the importance of well S in this investigation.   [1]

[Total: 6]

3 Copy and complete the following sentences by filling in missing words:

When temperature is increased up to the .... temperature for an enzyme, the activity of that enzyme will increase as the .... energy of molecules increases and more effective collisions occur. However, at temperatures higher than this, the enzyme is .... because the active site can no longer fit the .... Another factor that affects enzyme activity is ....

≪ RECALL AND CONNECT 2 ≪

Look back at Chapter 3: Movement into and out of cells. Compare the motion of solute particles in a cold solution with a hot solution. Assume both solutions have the same concentration of solute.

REFLECTION

How did you find the question containing both the 'predict' and 'explain' command words? Did you find it easy to structure your response? Check your answer against the one provided – did you score all **four** marks? How could you improve your answer so that both elements of the question are answered fully?

SELF-ASSESSMENT CHECKLIST

Let's revisit the Knowledge focus and Exam skills focus for this chapter.

Decide how confident you are with each statement.

Now I can:	Show it	Needs more work	Almost there	Confident to move on
understand about enzymes and how they work as catalysts	Draw a diagram to show how the active site is important in an enzyme-catalysed reaction.			
investigate how temperature and pH affect the activity of enzymes	Carry out an investigation on how temperature and pH affect the activity of enzymes and explain the results.			
find out why enzymes are specific and why temperature and pH affect them	Draw a diagram that shows how denaturation of an enzyme prevents it from working properly.			
understand the 'predict' and 'explain' command words.	Explain to a friend what the command words 'predict' and 'explain' mean.			

6 Plant nutrition

In this chapter, you will practise your understanding of the command word 'suggest' and how to answer questions that start with this command word. You will also compare it to the command word 'explain'.

Suggest	apply knowledge and understanding to situations where there is a range of valid responses to make proposals/put forward considerations.

The 'suggest' command word can be used in two different ways: where there is not a conclusive answer to the question, or where you need to draw upon wider knowledge to deal with an unfamiliar context. This type of question usually requires higher-order thinking skills such as analysis, critical thinking and problem solving. You will be able to practise answering this type of 'suggest' question in this chapter.

6.1 Making carbohydrates using light energy

⟪ RECALL AND CONNECT 1 ⟪

Look back at Chapter 1: Characteristics and classification of living organisms. Photosynthesis is the process through which plants obtain nutrition. Define the term 'nutrition'.

1   Plants use a process called photosynthesis to make organic molecules from inorganic components.

   a   Write the word equation for photosynthesis.

   b   The photosynthesis reaction requires energy. Where does this come from and how do plants capture it?

UNDERSTAND THIS TERM
• photosynthesis

2   Leaves that photosynthesise produce glucose. This is then turned into other substances.

   a   Figure 6.1 shows a variegated leaf and a leaf (on the right) that has had its chlorophyll removed and been stained with iodine solution. State the name of the molecule that this image shows has been produced in the leaf.   [1]

UNDERSTAND THESE TERMS
• sucrose
• nectar

Figure 6.1

   b   Suggest why is it useful to the plant that the molecule produced is insoluble.   [2]

   c   Explain why the plant turn starch into sucrose to allow it to be transported.   [2]

[Total: 5]

3 Plants carry out photosynthesis to make nutrient molecules.

a Copy and complete the table with the information about the molecules that are produced from glucose by plants.

Molecule		amino acids	
Use	attract pollinators		capture light energy
Ion needed	none		

[3]

b Suggest why different carbohydrates are produced as part of photosynthesis. [1]

[Total: 4]

REFLECTION

How confident are you that you know what the command word 'suggest' means? How is it different from the command word 'explain'? Look back at your answer for the 'suggest' Question 3b and make sure you have not stated a fact but have instead applied your knowledge of this chapter and others to the question.

4 A student investigated the effect of nitrate ion concentration on common duckweed (*Lemna minor*). They set up dishes containing 20 *L. minor* plants at varying concentrations of nitrate ions. They counted the number of plants after 25 days and noted their appearance. The results are shown in the following table:

Concentration of nitrate salt/mg dm^{-3}	Number of plants	Appearance of plants
0.00	18	yellowish small leaves
0.05	24	yellowish small leaves
0.10	45	normal appearance
0.20	90	normal appearance
0.30	91	normal appearance

a Describe the effect of increasing nitrate concentration on *L. minor* growth using the information in the table. [3]

b Explain the effect of increasing nitrate concentration from 0.00 mg dm^{-3} to 0.20 mg dm^{-3}. [3]

c Suggest a reason why the number of plants does not increase much between concentrations of 0.20 and 0.30 mg dm^{-3}. [1]

[Total: 7]

REFLECTION

'Suggest' questions are often used when data do not seem to fit an obvious pattern. There might be multiple correct answers to such a question.
Do you think your suggestion gives a valid possible answer to the question?

5   Four test tubes are set up as in Figure 6.2. Tubes B and D contain an aquatic plant and tubes C and D contain an aquatic snail.

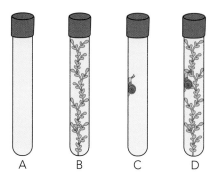

Figure 6.2: Experiment to investigate the effect of an aquatic plant and an aquatic snail on dissolved oxygen in water

a   What is the function of tube A?

b   Which tube is going to have the most dissolved oxygen after having been left for 6 hours in a lit area? Explain why.

c   Which tube will have the least dissolved oxygen? Explain why.

6.2 Leaf structure

≪ RECALL AND CONNECT 2 ≪

Look back at Chapter 3: Movement into and out of cells. Gases move into and out of the leaf by diffusion. What are the factors that affect the rate of diffusion of a substance?

UNDERSTAND THESE TERMS

- vascular bundle
- palisade mesophyll
- spongy mesophyll

1   Figure 6.3 shows a cross-section of a leaf from a dicotyledonous plant.

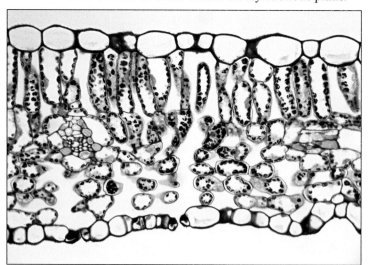

Figure 6.3

a   State the function of the air spaces in the spongy mesophyll.   [1]

b   Explain two adaptations of a leaf, visible in Figure 6.3, which make it well adapted to carrying out photosynthesis.   [2]

c   Suggest why most terrestrial plants have their stomata on the bottom of the leaf.   [2]

[Total: 5]

2   Figure 6.4 shows a cross-section of a leaf.

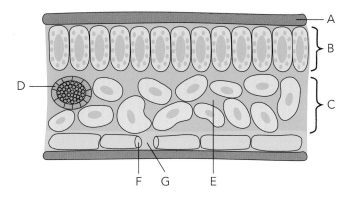

Figure 6.4: Diagram of a cross-section of a leaf

Write down the letter and name of the cell or tissue as answers to each of the following statements.

a   The cells that secrete a waxy substance that will form the cuticle.

b   The cells that control the movement of gases into and out of the leaf.

c   The tissue that is the main site of photosynthesis.

d   The structure that contains xylem vessels.

6.3 Factors affecting photosynthesis

1   You need to be able to plan an experiment investigating the necessity of certain factors for photosynthesis.

a   Plan an experiment to allow you to investigate the necessity of chlorophyll for photosynthesis.

b   You should ensure that your experiment has a control experiment with it. What is meant by the term 'control'?

c   How can you ensure that any starch produced in your experiment is the result of your actions rather than it already being present?

UNDERSTAND THESE TERMS

- destarching
- control

2 Researchers in 1984 looked at the effect of increasing the temperature and carbon dioxide concentration on the Big-tooth aspen, *Populus grandidentata*. They looked at two carbon dioxide concentrations. The results are shown in Figure 6.5. The blue line represents a carbon dioxide concentration that is much higher than the atmospheric concentration (1935 ppm), while the black line represented the atmospheric concentration of carbon dioxide at the time (325 ppm).

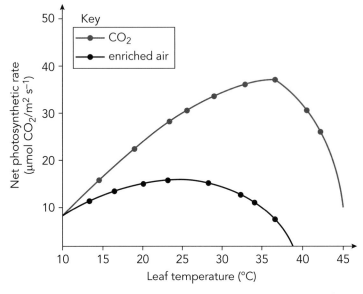

Figure 6.5

a Describe how the change in concentration affected the rate of photosynthesis over time using data from Figure 6.5 in your answer. [3]

b Explain why the rate of photosynthesis at the higher temperatures increases between 10 and 37°C but decreases between 37 and 45°C. [4]

c Suggest and explain, using the results in Figure 6.5, what the effect of the increasing atmospheric carbon dioxide levels since 1984 to 418 ppm in 2022 has had on plant growth. [5]

[Total: 12]

REFLECTION

Some of the highest demand questions in exams are those that link 'suggest' and 'explain'. Here you will have to apply your knowledge and then use it to back up your suggestion using the scientific information you have learnt. You need to do both to gain full marks. Look back at your answer for Question 2c in this section and consider whether you have 'suggested' the effect as well as 'explained' why this effect would happen.

3 A student set up the experiment in Figure 6.6 to investigate the effect of changing the light intensity on the rate at which the pondweed (*Egeria densa*) produced bubbles.

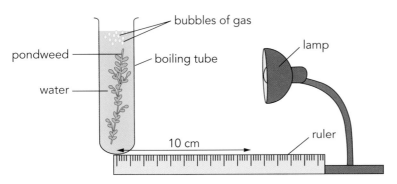

Figure 6.6

a State the gas produced by the *Egeria*. [1]

b The student's results are shown in the following table:

Distance of bulb from plant/cm	Number of bubbles produced per minute
5	46
15	45
25	32
35	18
45	5

Describe and explain how the distance of the bulb from the plant affected the rate of photosynthesis. [4]

c Suggest and explain two improvements the student could make to increase the accuracy of the experimental set-up. [4]

[Total: 9]

SELF-ASSESSMENT CHECKLIST

Let's revisit the Knowledge focus and Exam skills focus for this chapter.

Decide how confident you are with each statement.

Now I can:	Show it	Needs more work	Almost there	Confident to move on
understand photosynthesis and recall the equation for it	State the word equation for photosynthesis.			
find out how plants use the carbohydrates made in photosynthesis	Name four molecules that the plant makes from glucose and describe their uses within the plant.			
understand how the structure of a leaf is adapted for photosynthesis	Draw a labelled diagram of a cross-section of a leaf.			
investigate the need for chlorophyll, light and carbon dioxide in photosynthesis	Plan an experiment that demonstrates the need for light in photosynthesis.			
investigate how light, carbon dioxide and temperature affect the rate of photosynthesis	Describe the effect of carbon dioxide concentration on the rate of photosynthesis.			
understand the 'suggest' command word.	Discuss with a friend the difference between the 'suggest' and the 'explain' command words when used in an exam-style question.			

7 Human nutrition

The command term 'identify' requires a decision to be made about the location or name of a particular biological process or structure. For example, you might be asked to draw a label line or a cross on a diagram, or you could be asked to name organs in the body, or structures in a plant leaf from diagrams or images.

You may be asked to select the correct choice from a selection of possible answers, or to interpret trends from a graph. Answers to 'identify' questions are often short responses, similar to the answers for 'state' or 'give' questions. When you answer the 'identify' questions in this chapter, be clear in your responses and spell key terms correctly.

Identify	name, select or recognise.

7.1 Diet

1 What is a 'balanced diet'?

2 Why do nutrient deficiency disorders apply to some components of the balanced diet more than others?

3 Vegans are people who choose not to eat animal products such as meat, eggs and milk. Some vegans will take dietary supplements to increase their intake of components of a balanced diet. Suggest three of these components and a principal source for each that would be suitable for vegans. **[Total: 6]**

> **UNDERSTAND THESE TERMS**
>
> - carbohydrate
> - fibre
> - protein
> - rickets
> - scurvy
> - vitamin

> **《 RECALL AND CONNECT 1 《**
>
> Look back at Chapter 4: Biological molecules. List the biological molecules you have previously encountered in your course. What are the laboratory procedures that you can use to test for them and what are the positive results you would use to confirm their presence?

7.2 The human digestive system

1 Arrange the following terms in the order in which they occur in the human digestive system: absorption, assimilation, digestion and ingestion.

2 Construct a table showing the similarities and differences in the functions of the small and large intestines.

3 Figure 7.1 shows the processes occurring during a period of two and a half hours in the part of the human digestive system containing the stomach.

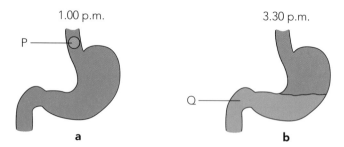

1.00 p.m.   3.30 p.m.

P   Q

a   b

Figure 7.1

a Identify the structures through which the food labelled P and Q is passing. [2]

b The food at P and Q is different in terms of the biological molecules it contains.

　　i State one difference between the molecules in the food at P from the food at Q. [1]

　　ii Explain your answer to **bi**. [1]

　　iii State one similarity between the molecules in the food at P and the food at Q. [1]

c Some people find it difficult to lose weight. Figure 7.2 shows a form of weight loss treatment called gastric bypass surgery.

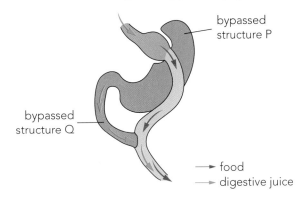

Figure 7.2: A stomach that has been subject to gastric bypass surgery

In gastric bypass surgery a small section of the stomach is connected with a part of the small intestine.

Suggest how gastric bypass surgery can help people to lose weight. [3]

[Total: 8]

≪ RECALL AND CONNECT 2 ≪

Look back at Chapter 2: Cells. Arrange these terms in the correct order from smallest to largest: tissue, organ, cell, organ system.

REFLECTION

How well do you think you can remember the order of structures through which food passes on its journey along the alimentary canal? What techniques could you use to help you?

UNDERSTAND THESE TERMS

- alimentary canal
- egestion
- gall bladder
- ingestion
- liver
- pancreas

7.3 Digestion

1 Copy and complete the following sentences using appropriate terms:

.... acid in the stomach kills pathogens and provides the optimum pH for the enzyme .... to digest protein into .... However, the .... pH for other enzymes in the digestive system, such as ...., is higher than this.

2 Figure 7.3 shows a simplified diagram of the process of a type of enzyme called a protease.

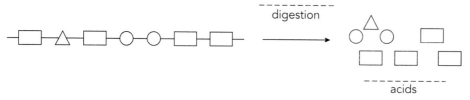

Figure 7.3: The action of the enzyme protease on a protein

    a Identify the two missing words in Figure 7.3.   [2]

    b Suggest how a diagram that shows the effect of amylase on starch would appear different.   [1]

    c Explain why exposure of lipids to bile is necessary for their effective chemical digestion.   [3]

           [Total: 6]

3 Physical processes are also an important part of digestion and involve the teeth. Identify the labels on the diagram of the tooth in Figure 7.4.

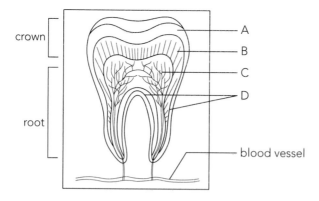

Figure 7.4: A human tooth

≪ RECALL AND CONNECT 3 ≪

Think back to Chapter 5: Enzymes. Can you draw a labelled diagram to show how an enzyme catalyses the breakdown of a larger molecule (substrate) into two smaller molecules (products)?

UNDERSTAND THESE TERMS

- amylase
- bile
- dentine
- emulsification
- incisor
- optimum

REFLECTION

Humans have four types of teeth: incisors, canines, premolars and molars. Can you think of any ways in which you can remember their shapes, functions and position in the mouth?

7.4 Absorption and assimilation

1   How is water absorbed in the intestines?

2   Why would assimilation not be possible without successful absorption?

3   Absorption occurs in the ileum section of the small intestine. Its efficiency is increased by the shape of the structures labelled X shown in Figure 7.5.

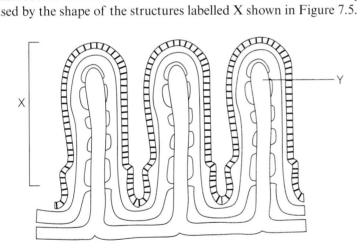

Figure 7.5

a   Identify the structures labelled X in Figure 7.5 and explain how their shape increases the efficiency of absorption.   [3]

b Label Y identifies an important structure involved in the absorption of the products of lipid digestion.

    i State the name of structure Y. [1]

    ii Describe the process by which the products of lipid digestion are absorbed into structure Y. [2]

[Total: 6]

≪ RECALL AND CONNECT 4 ≪

Look back at Chapter 3: Movement into and out of cells. List the processes by which substances can move into and out of cells. How do they compare?

UNDERSTAND THESE TERMS

- assimilation
- colon
- lacteal
- microvilli
- villi

REFLECTION

The different structures found within a microvillus have specific functions. How well do you think you can recall which function corresponds to which structure?

SELF-ASSESSMENT CHECKLIST

Let's revisit the Knowledge focus and Exam skills focus for this chapter.

Decide how confident you are with each statement.

Now I can:	Show it	Needs more work	Almost there	Confident to move on
describe what is meant by a balanced diet	Draw a mind map to show the components of a balanced diet. Add branches to each component to list items of food that provide good sources and the names of any deficiency diseases.			
describe the structure and function of the digestive system	Construct a table with two columns, with 'Structure' as the heading of the left column and 'Function' as the heading of the right column. Fill your table with information relating to the human digestive system. For example, 'salivary gland' may be accompanied by 'secretes saliva, contains the enzyme amylase'.			

CONTINUED

Now I can:	Show it	Needs more work	Almost there	Confident to move on
explain how and where physical and chemical digestion happen	Produce a fishbone diagram that shows the structures and substances that bring about physical and chemical digestion.			
summarise information using an annotated drawing	Draw a simple diagram of the human digestive system.			
understand what knowledge you need to demonstrate	List the order of structures in the digestive system through which food passes on its journey from the mouth to the anus.			
present knowledge clearly and coherently	Describe the role of bile in the human digestive system.			
understand how to answer questions with the 'identify' command word	Write a question and mark scheme on a topic from this chapter using the 'identify' command word.			
develop strategies that help you recall concepts and information.	Apply the technique(s) you have identified to help you answer a past paper question on this topic.			

Exam practice 2

This section contains past paper questions from previous Cambridge exams, which draw together your knowledge on a range of topics that you have covered up to this point. These questions give you the opportunity to test your knowledge and understanding. Additional past paper practice questions can be found in the accompanying digital material.

The following question has an example student response and commentary provided. Once you have worked through the question, read the student response and commentary. Are your answers different to the example response?

1 The manufacturers of health drink **H** claim that it contains protein and glucose.

Describe how you would test health drink **H** for protein and glucose. Include the results for a positive test.

protein:

glucose: **[Total: 5]**

Cambridge IGCSE Biology (0610) Paper 63 Q1c, June 2021

Example student response	Commentary
1 I would test the drink with biuret solution to see if there's any protein. This is a blue solution that will go colourless when there's protein present. I would test the drink with Benedict's solution to test for glucose as it is a reducing sugar. If glucose is present the mixture will go from blue to brick red.	The student made a good attempt at this question but did not note the number of marks available. There is a factual error in the test for protein and the student is possibly confused with the test for vitamin C with DCPIP. Biuret solution will go from blue to lilac in the presence of protein. One mark is gained for this part. The second part is correct but lacking in detail. Adding Benedict's solution will not turn the solution brick red without heating the mixture first. This is the missing marking point. *This answer is awarded 3 out of 5 marks.*

The following question has an example student response and commentary provided. Once you have read and answered the questions, read the student response and commentary and compare your answers. Are your answers different? If they are, how are the different?

2 Phloem is used to transport sucrose and amino acids in plants. Sucrose is a carbohydrate. Describe the uses of carbohydrates **and** amino acids in plants. **[Total: 4]**

Cambridge IGCSE Biology (0610) Paper 41 Q2a, November 2019

Example student response	Commentary
2 Carbohydrates can be used for various things in plants. Some glucose undergoes respiration to release energy, allowing the plant to carry out work such as active transport and synthesising larger molecules. One such large molecule is starch, a glucose polymer, used by the plant as a storage molecule and which will be broken down later to release maltose and glucose for respiration. Another large molecule is cellulose which is used to produce the cell walls in plants and is also a polymer of glucose. Glucose is converted to sucrose by adding it to fructose. Sucrose is transported in the plant through the phloem and is used in the production of nectar in the flowers.	The student wrote an excellent answer on the uses of carbohydrates in plants and would easily gain four marks if that was the question. However, the question asks for the uses of carbohydrates and amino acids. They should have included how amino acids are used in plants and mentioned a named protein that is found in plants. The mention of a human protein (such as an antibody or insulin) would not have gained them the mark. *This answer is awarded 2 out of 4 marks.*

3 Now you have read the commentary, write an improved answer to the sections where you lost marks. Use the commentary to guide you as you improve your answers.

The following question has an example student commentary and answer provided. Work through the question first, then compare your answer to the sample answer and commentary.

4 The rate of photosynthesis of parts of individual leaves can be measured using a hand-held device as shown in Fig 4.1. This apparatus allows air to flow through the transparent chamber that encloses part of the leaf. The apparatus measures the carbon dioxide concentration of the air entering and leaving the chamber.

transparent chamber

Fig 4.1

a   A student used the apparatus shown in Fig 4.1 to investigate the effect of temperature on the rate of photosynthesis of the leaves of Chinese plantain, *Plantago asiatica*, at two different concentrations of carbon dioxide, **A** and **B**. Fig 4.2 shows the results of the investigation.

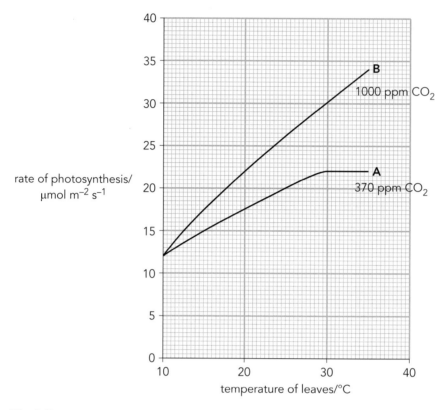

Fig 4.2

i   State **one** environmental factor that should have been kept constant in this investigation. [1]

ii   Describe the effect of temperature on the rate of photosynthesis when carbon dioxide concentration A was supplied.
Use the data from Fig 4.2 in your answer. [3]

iii   Calculate the percentage increase in the rate of photosynthesis at 30°C when the carbon dioxide concentration was increased from A to B as shown in Fig 4.2.
Show your working and give your answer to the nearest whole number. [2]

iv   Explain the effect of increasing temperature on the rate of photosynthesis for carbon dioxide concentration B.
Use the term '*limiting factor*' in your answer. [3]

v The student concluded that carbon dioxide concentration is the factor limiting the rate of photosynthesis between 30°C and 35°C for the results shown for A in Fig 4.2.

State the evidence for this conclusion.   [1]

[Total: 10]

Cambridge IGCSE Biology (0610) Paper 41 Q2c, June 2019

Example student response			Commentary		
4	**a**	**i** Light	**a**	**i**	This answer is incorrect due to its lack of precision – it should be light intensity. Humidity or water supply could also have been answers. *This answer is awarded 0 out of 1 mark.*
	ii	The rate of photosynthesis increases and then levels off.		**ii**	The student should have mentioned that the graph levels off at 30°C and that the rate increases from 10 to 20 µmol per m² per s between 10 and 30°C. *This answer is awarded 1 out of 3 marks.*
	iii	The percentage increase is the difference in the rate divided by the value of A. 30 – 22 = 8. 8 divided by 22 is 0.36. To turn this into a percentage makes 36%.		**iii**	This is correct and shows the working in full. *This answer is awarded 2 out of 2 marks.*
	iv	Temperature is the limiting factor over the whole range. Carbon dioxide is not a limiting factor.		**iv**	The student did use the words 'limiting factor' but should have **explained** why the temperature was limiting. *This answer is awarded 2 out of 3 marks.*
	v	The rate of photosynthesis is higher at all temperatures when the carbon dioxide concentration is higher.		**v**	This answer is correct and describes the correlation well. *This answer is awarded 1 out of 1 mark.*

The following question is on similar topics. Use the information from the previous response and commentary to guide you as you answer.

5   Carbon dioxide may be collected from the burning of biofuel and sold for use in glasshouses. Explain why carbon dioxide is used in glasshouses. **[Total: 3]**

Adapted from Cambridge IGCSE Biology (0610) Paper 42 Q4b iv, November 2020

The following question has an example student commentary and answer provided. Work through the question first, then compare your answer to the sample answer and commentary. Are your answers different to the sample responses? What information does this give you about your understanding of this topic?

6 Fat is a necessary component of the human diet.

   a State **three** ways in which the human body uses fat. [3]

   The arrows in Fig 6.1 show the pathway of fat in part of the alimentary canal.

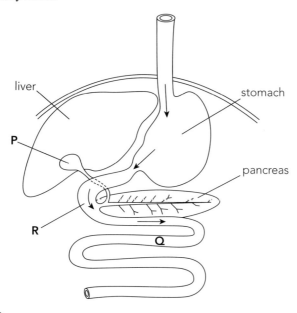

   Fig 6.1

   b State the name of:

   i the enzyme secreted by the pancreas that digests fat [1]

   ii the products of chemical digestion of fat [1]

   iii the liquid that is produced by the liver and stored by organ P in Fig 6.1 [1]

   iv organ P in Fig 6.1. [1]

   c Explain what happens to ingested fat at R in Fig 6.1 **before** chemical digestion occurs. [2]

   d Explain how the products of fat digestion are transported from **Q** to the rest of the body. [3]

   [Total: 12]

Cambridge IGCSE Biology (0610) Paper 41 Q1a–d, June 2017

Example student response	Commentary
6 a For energy release and storage and insulation.	The student correctly identifies the role of fat in energy release and storage, which attracts two marks. Their reference to insulation gains a third. *This answer is awarded 3 out of 3 marks.*
b i Lipase	This is the expected answer and the mark can be awarded. *This answer is awarded 1 out of 1 mark.*
ii Fatty acids and glycogen	The student correctly states that one product of fat digestion are fatty acids. However, the incorrect identification of glycogen, rather than glycerol, means that the student cannot gain this mark. *This answer is awarded 0 out of 1 mark.*
iii Enzymes	This is not the correct answer, the student should have given the answer bile. They cannot be awarded the mark. *This answer is awarded 0 out of 1 mark.*
iv Gall bladder	This is the expected answer and the mark can be awarded. *This answer is awarded 1 out of 1 mark.*
c It is chemically digested by the enzyme lipase. This happens when the pH increases.	The student does not refer to the process by which lipids undergo emulsification and how the surface area of droplets is increased. However, they can secure one mark for referring to the action of enzymes such as lipase. *This answer is awarded 1 out of 2 marks.*
d The products of fat digestion are transferred to the blood at Q. They are absorbed by microvilli, which provide a very high surface area for this purpose.	The student correctly states that the blood is the destination of the products of fat digestion and how they pass through the microvilli. However, there is neither reference to the role of lacteals, which are found inside villi, nor lymph, which is the fluid into which the products of fat digestion are absorbed. *This answer is awarded 2 out of 3 marks.*

7 Now that you've read through the commentary try writing a full mark scheme for Question **6**. This will help you understand the specific knowledge you are expected to show in your answers.

8 Transport in plants

KNOWLEDGE FOCUS

In this chapter you will answer questions on:

- xylem and phloem
- transport of water

 translocation of sucrose and amino acids.

EXAM SKILLS FOCUS

In this chapter you will:

- show that you can make connections between concepts and answer synoptic questions
- show that you understand the command word 'sketch' and answer a 'sketch' question.

Exam questions often require that you demonstrate knowledge from different topics and the connections between them. These are called synoptic questions. You need to make sure that you recognise when a question requires such connections to be made and how to demonstrate these in your answers. For example, questions related to this chapter will often contain material from Chapter 6: Plant nutrition as the processes are closely linked.

In this chapter you will also answer a question with the command word 'sketch'. Different types of plant structures, cells and enzymes are all examples of things you could be asked to 'sketch'. Sketches are expected to be simple and show the main features asked for by the question – draw your diagrams clearly and accurately but keep them simple.

Sketch	make a simple freehand drawing showing the key features, taking care over proportions.

8.1 Xylem and phloem

1 Plants need to move substances through their bodies just like humans do. This uses specialised tissues.

   Xylem and phloem make up the transport vessels in a plant.

   a What does each of the vessels carry?

   b How is the structure of xylem adapted to its function?

UNDERSTAND THIS TERM

   • lignin

2 Figure 8.1 shows the cross-section of a root of a buttercup plant.

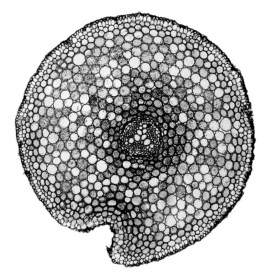

Figure 8.1: A cross-section of a root of a buttercup plant

   a Where is the vascular bundle located?

   b Make a drawing of the cross-section, labelling the xylem vessels.

3 Compare the differences between the function of xylem and phloem.   **[Total: 2]**

4 Scientists can test the rate at which water moves through a large plant by putting probes into a specific tissue of the plant.

   a State the name of this tissue.   [1]

   b Describe and explain how this tissue is adapted to its function.   [3]

   [Total: 4]

8.2 Transport of water

≪ RECALL AND CONNECT 2 ≪

Think back to Chapter 6: Plant nutrition. Plants absorb water and mineral ions such as nitrate and magnesium. What are these used for in the plant?

UNDERSTAND THESE TERMS

- transpiration
- transpiration pull

1   Water moves from the roots to the leaves along a specific pathway.

   a   How does water get from the soil into the xylem?

   b   How does the evaporation of water from leaf cells pull water up the xylem?

   c   What instrument would you use to measure transpiration rates?

2   Figure 8.2 shows the rate of water conduction through the xylem vessels of three different trees over a period of 24 hours.

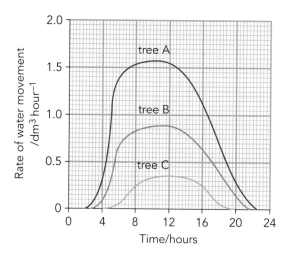

Figure 8.2

   a   Describe the shape of the graph for tree B using data from Figure 8.2.   [3]

   b   Explain how the scientists could calculate the total volume of water that has moved through tree B in this experiment.   [2]

   c   Suggest four reasons why the different trees might have a different rates of water conduction.   [4]

   [Total: 9]

8.3 Translocation of sucrose and amino acids

1   Water is not the only substance that needs to move throughout the plant. Some substances will move from the leaves to other tissues when the leaves are photosynthesising.

   a   What are two of the main substances that move from the leaf to other tissues?

   b   What is the name of this process?

   c   What are the roles of sources and sinks in the process?

UNDERSTAND THESE TERMS
• source
• sink

2   Figure 8.4 shows vascular bundles in the stem of a flowering plant.

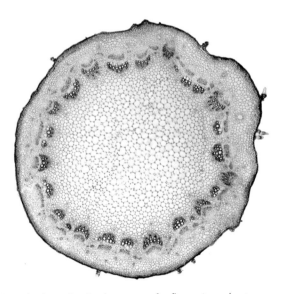

Figure 8.4: Vascular bundles in the stem of a flowering plant

   a   Sketch one of the bundles and label the xylem and phloem vessels.   [2]

   b   State the name of the substance transported in the phloem that requires nitrates to be absorbed from the soil.   [1]

   c   Explain why sucrose travels from the leaf to root at certain times of the year in this plant, but from the root to the shoot at other times.   [3]

   [Total: 6]

REFLECTION

Question 2 draws on your knowledge of the vascular bundles from Chapter 6: Plant nutrition as well as your practical drawing skills. Did you remember which biological molecule needs nitrogen and consider the life cycle of plants throughout a year? This is a high-demand question that needs a careful approach. Make sure you read the questions completely and note every word of the question. In Question 2b you may have been tempted to answer sucrose if you had not considered the word nitrates further along in the question. What can you do to ensure you approach questions like this carefully in the exam?

3   A tulip is a plant that regrows every year from a bulb, growing new leaves and a flower.

   a   When the plant is growing in early spring what are the source and sink for sucrose and amino acids and what will the plant do with these substances?

   b   Which tissues are the source and sink when the plant is fully grown and photosynthesising at a high rate?

SELF-ASSESSMENT CHECKLIST

Let's revisit the Knowledge focus and Exam skills focus for this chapter.

Decide how confident you are with each statement.

Now I can:	Show it	Needs more work	Almost there	Confident to move on
outline the functions of xylem and phloem and where they are found	Draw a cross-section of root and shoot and label the xylem and phloem vessels in each.			
describe the pathway taken by water as it moves throughout a plant	Make a flow chart showing the various tissues that water moves through from the soil to the atmosphere.			
investigate the movement of water through stems and leaves	Plan an experiment to investigate the flow of water through a celery plant.			
find out what transpiration is, why it happens and conditions that affect its rate	Plan an experiment to investigate the effect of wind speed on transpiration using a potometer.			
outline the translocation of sucrose and amino acids in plants	Describe how the movement of sucrose in phloem changes from spring to summer and autumn.			

CONTINUED

Now I can:	Show it	Needs more work	Almost there	Confident to move on
make connections between concepts and navigate synoptic questions	Look at exam questions in this book and identify the topics that are linked within them. Do the same with any other exam questions you have access to.			
understand the command word 'sketch' and answer a 'sketch' question.	Give the definition of the command word 'sketch'. Attempt to answer any 'sketch' question from a past paper.			

9 Transport in animals

It is common in IGCSE Biology examinations to be asked a question that requires you to 'calculate' a value using given data. For example, the 'calculate' question in this chapter presents two values and requires a percentage change calculation. Make sure you are familiar with examples of this type of question and the formulae you need to answer them.

| Calculate | work out from given facts, figures or information. |

9.1 Circulatory systems

1 What is a circulatory system?

2 A fish has a single circulatory system, which is different in structure
to the double circulatory system of a human.

    a Describe the single circulatory system in a fish. [1]

    b Explain why a septum is not required in a single circulatory system. [2]

    c Suggest one advantage of a double circulation. [1]

                                                       [Total: 4]

《 RECALL AND CONNECT 1 《

Look back at Chapter 7: Human nutrition. After the process of digestion in
humans, absorption happens. Where does this happen and why is it important?

UNDERSTAND THESE TERMS

- circulatory system
- double circulation
- single circulation

9.2 The heart

1 Why might too much fat in the diet cause coronary heart disease and how can
coronary heart disease be treated?

2 Around the heart there is a layer of tissue called the pericardium.
This can, in some people, become thicker because it contains too much fluid.
This condition is referred to as pericardial effusion. This is shown in Figure 9.1.

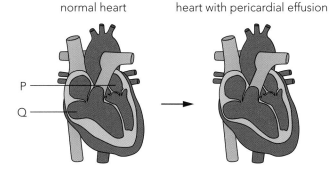

normal heart   heart with pericardial effusion

Figure 9.1

    a Identify chambers P and Q in Figure 9.1. [2]

    b A person with pericardial effusion cannot undertake intense physical
activity. Suggest why. [3]

    c Describe how a medical professional could determine the activity
of the heart. [1]

                                                         [Total: 6]

3 Complete the sentences with the missing words:

The heart pumps blood away in .... and returns it to the heart in .... Inside the heart, blood is kept flowing in the correct direction using one-way .... The left and right sides of the heart are separated by a structure called the ....

UNDERSTAND THESE TERMS
• atrium
• chamber
• septum
• valve
• ventricle

≪ RECALL AND CONNECT 2 ≪

Look back at Chapter 2: Cells. Muscle cells contain larger numbers of mitochondria. Why?

REFLECTION

The number of marks for each Exam skill question in this section varies from one to three marks. Do you feel confident that you understand what you are expected to include in your answers to these questions? How could you get more familiar with a mark scheme's expectations?

9.3 Blood vessels

1 a Construct a table showing the unique features of the three types of blood vessel.

b List the names of specific blood vessels you have learned (e.g. hepatic portal vein).

2 Figure 9.2 shows a simplified diagram of a part of the human circulatory system, with some of the blood vessels labelled.

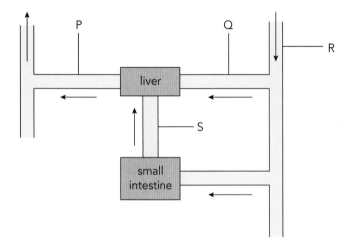

Figure 9.2: Simplified diagram of part of the human circulatory system

a Identify blood vessels P, Q, R and S on Figure 9.2. [4]

b Suggest **one** structural feature that all four vessels have in common. [1]

c   Describe **two** ways in which the structure of blood vessel P is different to that of blood vessel Q.   [2]

d   Suggest **one** way in which the blood in vessel P is different to that in vessel R.   [1]

[Total: 8]

3   Explain how the structure of a capillary helps it to fulfil its function.   **[Total: 2]**

‹‹ RECALL AND CONNECT 3 ‹‹

Look at Chapter 3: Movement into and out of cells. What are the differences between diffusion and active transport?

> ## UNDERSTAND THESE TERMS
>
> * artery
> * blood vessel
> * capillary
> * lumen
> * vein

REFLECTION

Humans have three types of blood vessel: arteries, veins and capillaries. There are some helpful ways to remember some of the most important aspects of them, for example, most **A**rteries carry blood **A**way from the heart; **V**eins have **V**alves. Can you think of any more examples?

9.4 Blood

1   Explain how this happens, with reference in your answer to fibrin and fibrinogen.

2   Blood circulates in vessels around the body and transports oxygen to respiring tissues.

a   Explain why the blood is described as a tissue.   [2]

b   The table below shows the different rates of blood flow to different parts in the human body at rest and during vigorous exercise.

Organ	Rate of blood flow/cm³ min⁻¹	
	at rest	during vigorous exercise
skin	350	1800
small intestine	950	450
skeletal muscles	950	9700

i   Calculate the percentage decrease in the rate of blood flow to the small intestine before and after exercise. Show your working and give your answer to the nearest whole number.   [2]

ii   Suggest reasons for the change in the rate of blood flow to the other two organs during vigorous exercise.   [4]

c   Other than oxygen transport, outline two other functions of the blood.   [2]

[Total: 10]

REFLECTION

How did you find the 'calculate' question? Did you know which calculation to use? The question includes two important instructions – did you identify these and apply them to your answer? How can you make sure you don't miss specific instructions like this when answering exam questions?

3 List the components that are carried in plasma.

UNDERSTAND THESE TERMS

- clotting
- plasma
- platelet
- red blood cell
- white blood cell

≪ RECALL AND CONNECT 4 ≪

Look at Chapter 7: Human nutrition. Why do humans need iron as part of a balanced diet?

4 Explain how phagocytes protect the body against infection. **[Total: 2]**

SELF-ASSESSMENT CHECKLIST

Let's revisit the Knowledge focus and Exam skills focus for this chapter.

Decide how confident you are with each statement.

Now I can:	Show it	Needs more work	Almost there	Confident to move on
describe the human circulatory system	Draw a mind map to show the components of the human circulatory system and how they relate to each other.			
describe the structure and function of the heart	Sketch a simple cross-sectional diagram of the heart. Add labels and then add an arrow to show the direction of blood through it.			
list factors that increase the risk of developing heart disease	Produce a fishbone diagram that shows the cause and effect of factors known to increase the risk of developing heart disease.			
investigate how exercise affects heart rate	Draw a flow diagram to show how exercise affects heart rate.			

CONTINUED

Now I can:	Show it	Needs more work	Almost there	Confident to move on
compare the structure and function of arteries, veins and capillaries	Draw a Venn diagram to show the similarities and differences between the structure and function of arteries, veins and capillaries. You may wish to draw the cross-sectional structures of the vessels as the circles in your diagram.			
describe the components of blood and what they do	Draw a table to show the components of blood and what they do.			
explain how the structures of arteries, veins and capillaries are related to their functions	Write a short paragraph to explain how the structures of arteries, veins and capillaries are related to their functions. Ensure you include the word 'because' as much as possible.			
show that I understand how to answer questions with the command word 'calculate'.	Find some 'calculate' questions in past papers and check that you know which calculation or formula you would need to use for each.			

10 Diseases and immunity

In a multiple-choice question, the answer will be one of the options provided. But it will be 'hidden' among a number of distractors (answers that may seem correct if you do not think about them).

So, when answering multiple-choice questions, it is a good idea to use the 'elimination method'. Even if you think you know the answer, double check by reading all the options and eliminating the ones that are incorrect. Take extra care over the distractors.

10.1 Transmission of pathogens

UNDERSTAND THESE TERMS

- host
- transmission

1   Pathogens are disease-causing organisms that can be passed from one individual
to another.

    a   What are the different ways in which a pathogen can be transmitted from
one host to another?

    b   How can pathogens cause disease symptoms in their host?

    c   What does the body use as defences to stop the pathogen from getting
into the blood?

2   Our body can protect us against disease but it is more useful to prevent the
organisms from growing in the first place. There are various actions that can
be taken by society and by individuals to prevent the spread of pathogens.

    a   You can get diseases such as *Salmonella* poisoning from food that has not
been prepared in a safe way. What are the four ways in which food hygiene
can be improved?

    b   Why are the development of a working sewage system and treatment
facilities important in the prevention of the spread of disease?

3   Which of the following diseases is transmissible?

    A   The common cold, caused by a virus.

    B   Sickle-cell anaemia, caused by a genetic mutation.

    C   Coronary heart disease, caused by a build-up of fat in the arteries.

    D   Lung cancer, caused by exposure to asbestos fibres.   **[Total: 1]**

REFLECTION

The questions in this section of the book are mostly short-answer questions.
These questions can range from one to four marks and start with a specific
command word. Compare them to multiple-choice questions. How are these
different? Do you approach them in a different manner?

10.2 The immune response

<< RECALL AND CONNECT 2 <<

There are several different types of white blood cells as seen in Chapter 9: Transport in animals. What is the difference between phagocytes and lymphocytes?

UNDERSTAND THESE TERMS

• antigen
• active immunity

1 The immune system will be able to target specific pathogens and form lifelong immunity to these organisms.

a How do lymphocytes target specific pathogens?

b Why do you develop immunity to a disease after you have been exposed to the pathogen?

c What is the difference between passive and active immunity?

d How can a vaccination programme prevent the spread of an infectious disease?

2 Figure 10.1 shows the prevalence of Human Papilloma Virus (HPV) amongst females aged 16–18 over a period. HPV can cause cervical cancer in females. In 2008, a programme to start the vaccination of 12–13-year-old girls was first started.

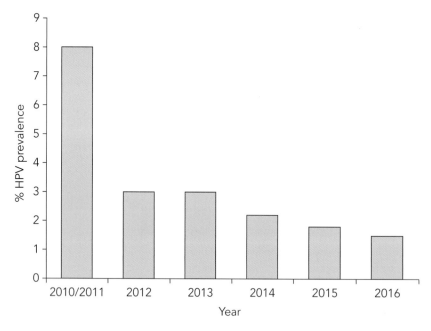

Figure 10.1: Prevalence of Human Papilloma Virus (HPV) amongst females

a Describe the graph using data from Figure 10.1. [3]

b Explain why the prevalence of HPV has decreased from 2012 onwards, using your knowledge of vaccinations. [4]

c   Cervical cancer is most commonly diagnosed in females aged 30–34.
Suggest and explain what is going to happen to cervical cancer cases
from 2025 onwards.   [3]

[Total: 10]

3   How long does it take lymphocytes to start making large amounts of antibodies?

A   a few minutes

B   a few hours

C   a few days

D   a few weeks   **[Total: 1]**

REFLECTION

Short-answer questions in Biology can vary in length. At their simplest, they
are recall questions asking for a simple definition for one mark. Questions that
ask you to analyse data or explain a complex pathway may have four or
five marks. Look at the number of marks available for a question and tailor
your answer accordingly to avoid losing marks.

SELF-ASSESSMENT CHECKLIST

Let's revisit the Knowledge focus and Exam skills focus for this chapter.

Decide how confident you are with each statement.

Now I can:	Show it	Needs more work	Almost there	Confident to move on
find out how pathogens are transmitted from one host to another	Make a table showing the different methods of direct and indirect transmission and find examples of each type.			
outline how the body defends itself against pathogens	Make a flow chart showing the passive and active defences of the body. Can you explain how the body can prevent a pathogen from getting in?			

CONTINUED

Now I can:	Show it	Needs more work	Almost there	Confident to move on
explain what immunity is and how it is produced naturally and through vaccination	Write the words antigen, antibody, pathogen, vaccine, lymphocyte, memory lymphocyte on a piece of paper. Can you add arrows and labels to show how the words are linked?			
understand how to approach multiple-choice questions.	Explain to a friend how you would approach a multiple-choice question and why.			

Exam practice 3

This section contains past paper questions from previous Cambridge exams, which draw together your knowledge on a range of topics that you have covered up to this point. These questions give you the opportunity to test your knowledge and understanding. Additional past paper practice questions can be found in the accompanying digital material.

The following question has an example student response and commentary provided. Once you have worked through the question, read the student response and commentary. Are your answers different to the example response?

1   Aphids are used by investigators to discover how plants transport sucrose.

Fig 1.1 shows an aphid with its mouthparts inserted into a plant stem to feed on the liquid in the phloem.

A plant was put in a dark cupboard for several days. Four aphids, **A**, **B**, **C** and **D**, were then placed on a different plant in the dark cupboard as shown in Fig 1.2.

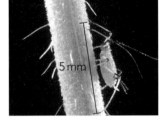

Fig 1.1

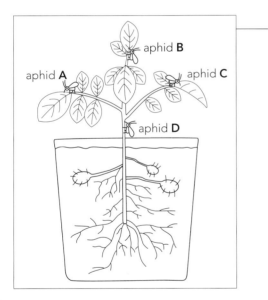

Fig 1.2

Immediately after the aphids were placed on the plant it was observed that:

*   all the aphids ingested the same volume of liquid from the phloem

*   aphid **D** ingested the highest concentration of sucrose.

Explain why aphid **D** ingested the highest concentration of sucrose.   **[Total: 3]**

Cambridge IGCSE Biology (0610) Paper 41 Q2ci, November 2019

Example student response	Commentary
1 Aphid D gets more sucrose as it is on the stem rather than on one of the branches. This means it gets all of the sucrose from all of the branches. This sucrose is travelling through translocation in the phloem.	The student has realised that this is a question about translocation and that sucrose moves through this process. This gains one mark. They have misinterpreted the question though as the plant is in the dark. As such, the leaves are not photosynthesising and are not the source of the sucrose. *This answer is awarded 1 out of 3 marks.*

2   Now that you've gone through the commentary, write an improved answer to parts of question 1 where you did not score highly. Use the commentary to guide you as you answer.

The following question has an example student response and commentary provided.

Once you have read and answered the questions, read the student response and commentary and compare your answers. Are your answers different? If they are, how are the different?

3   A scientist investigated the effect of temperature on the mass of leaves picked from a tea plant, *Camellia sinensis*.

   •   Three samples of leaves were picked and the mass of each sample of leaves was recorded.

   •   Each sample of leaves was kept at a different temperature for four hours.

   •   After four hours, the mass of each sample of leaves was measured and recorded again.

   •   The scientist then calculated the final mass as a percentage of the initial mass for each sample.

Fig 3.1 shows the results.

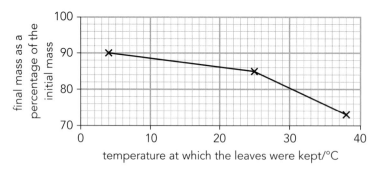

Fig 3.1

Explain the results shown in Fig 3.1.   **[Total: 5]**

Cambridge IGCSE Biology (0610) Paper 42 Q3a i, March 2022

Example student response	Commentary
3 The mass of the leaves decreases as the temperature increases. This is because as the temperature goes up the rate of transpiration increases and water vapour flows through the stomata.	The student would get a mark for stating the correlation, another for linking this to the rate of transpiration and a final one for the description of the loss of water vapour through the stomata. To improve, they could have included a description of the evaporation of water from the mesophyll cells (for two further marks), mentioned the word diffusion rather than flow and discussed the increased kinetic energy of the particles at higher temperatures. *This answer is awarded 3 out of 5 marks.*

Now attempt this next question on a similar topic. Use your previous answers, the sample responses and commentaries to guide you as you answer.

4   a   Fig 4.1 shows the human heart and the main blood vessels. The functions of the parts of the heart and some of the blood vessels are given in Table 4.1.

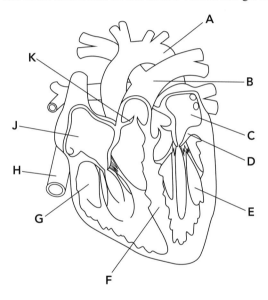

Fig 4.1

Copy and complete Table 4.1. One row has been done for you. [6]

function	letter on Fig 4.1	name
structure that separates oxygenated and deoxygenated blood		
structure that prevents backflow of blood from ventricle to atrium		
blood vessel that carries oxygenated blood	A	aorta
blood vessel that carries deoxygenated blood		
structure that prevents backflow of blood from pulmonary artery to right ventricle		
chamber of the heart that contains oxygenated blood		
chamber of the heart that contains deoxygenated blood		

Table 4.1

b   A group of students used a heart monitor to record the pulse rate of an athlete during a 5000 metre race. The recordings started just before the race began and ended just after it had finished, as shown in Fig 4.2.

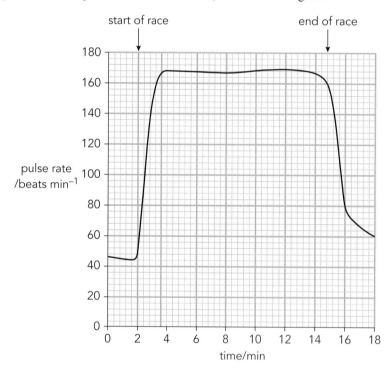

i   Use data from Fig 4.2 to describe the effect of exercise on the pulse rate of the athlete. [3]

ii Explain the change in pulse rate between 2 minutes and 3 minutes after the recordings started. [4]

[Total: 13]

Cambridge IGCSE Biology (0610) Paper 41 Q1, June 2016

The following question has an example student commentary and answer provided. Work through the question first, then compare your answer to the sample answer and commentary. Are your answers different to the sample responses? What information does this give you about your understanding of this topic?

5   a   Antibodies are proteins that are produced by lymphocytes. Antitoxins are antibodies which neutralise the toxins released by some bacteria.

The transmissible disease diphtheria is caused by a bacterium that releases a toxin that can cause serious damage to the body.

A person is suspected of having caught diphtheria.

At a clinic, the person is given an injection of antitoxin antibodies that provide protection against the diphtheria toxin. She is also given an injection of the vaccine for diphtheria.

A few weeks later she is given a second injection of the diphtheria vaccine.

Fig 5.1 shows the changes in concentration of the antitoxin antibodies and the antibodies produced in response to the vaccine.

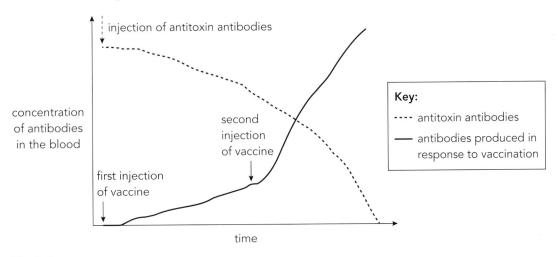

Fig 5.1

i   Explain the advantage of giving the person an injection of antitoxin antibodies. [2]

ii   Explain how the two injections of the vaccine result in better protection against diphtheria than the injection of antitoxin antibodies. [3]

b   Explain how antibodies protect the body against pathogens. [4]

[Total: 9]

Cambridge IGCSE Biology (0610) Paper 41 Q6a, b, June 2021

Example student response	Commentary
5 a i This gives the person immediate immunity to the disease.	**a i** This is the correct answer but the student did not use the key terminology that is expected in this answer (**passive immunity**) and as a result, only one mark can be awarded for the use of the word immediate. *This answer is awarded 1 out of 2 marks.*
ii Vaccination is a form of active immunity which will give longer-term protection.	**ii** Here the student uses the key term **active immunity**, gaining them one mark. A second mark is gained for saying that this is a long-term protection. However, the third mark cannot be awarded because this process is not explained. The student should have mentioned memory cells or the secondary immune response to gain the third mark. *This answer is awarded 2 out of 3 marks.*
b Antibodies can bind to pathogens and stop them from working. This is because the antibody binds to the antigen on the pathogen.	**b** Again, the student's response lacks the detail required to **explain** the question. Two marks can be awarded for stating that pathogens have antigens and the antibodies will bind to them. The missing explanation is that the antibody is specific (or has a complementary shape) to the antigen and marks the pathogen for destruction by phagocytes. *This answer is awarded 2 out of 4 marks.*

The following two questions are on similar topics. Use the information from the previous response and commentary to guide you as you answer.

6 Describe **and** explain the effects of cholera bacteria on the gut. **[Total: 4]**

Cambridge IGCSE Biology (0610) Paper 42 Q1di, March 2018

7 The body has defence mechanisms to protect it from infection.

Outline the body's defence mechanisms. **[Total: 5]**

Cambridge IGCSE Biology (0610) Paper 41 Q4a, November 2019

11 Respiration and gas exchange

KNOWLEDGE FOCUS

In this chapter you will answer questions on:

- respiration
- gas exchange in humans.

EXAM SKILLS FOCUS

In this chapter you will:

- consider how to distribute time across the whole paper.

Time management in exams is an important skill. To help you to effectively manage your time, consider how many marks are allocated to each question. As you attempt the exam-style questions in this chapter, check you have provided enough information and detail to satisfy the number of marks and note how long it takes you to answer these questions. You should check the total number of marks across a whole paper to work out how many minutes you should be spending per mark. Keep an eye on time when you are practising the exam-style questions in this chapter.

11.1 Respiration

1 Respiration, a process that releases chemical energy in cells, is one of the seven characteristics of life. It requires glucose and sometimes oxygen.

   a   Why do cells need energy? Give two reasons.

   b   What is one source of glucose in the human body?

   c   How is oxygen transported to respiring cells in the human body?

2 Respiration can be aerobic or anaerobic.

   a   Copy and complete Table 11.1 to distinguish between aerobic and anaerobic respiration in humans and yeast.

Species	Type of respiration	Reactant(s)	Product(s)
humans	aerobic		
	anaerobic		
yeast	anaerobic		

Table 11.1

[6]

   b   Describe one other difference, not shown in Table 11.1, between aerobic respiration and anaerobic respiration in humans. [1]

[Total: 7]

3 a   Explain what is meant by the term 'oxygen debt'. [2]

   b   Describe the processes that involve the lactic acid produced during anaerobic respiration in humans. [2]

[Total: 4]

> ## ≪ RECALL AND CONNECT 1 ≪
>
> Look back at Chapter 5: Enzymes. Which factors control enzyme-catalysed reactions such as those that occur in respiration?

UNDERSTAND THESE TERMS

- aerobic
- anaerobic
- energy
- lactic acid
- oxygen debt

REFLECTION

There are many similarities and differences between aerobic respiration and anaerobic respiration. There are also many similarities and differences between anaerobic respiration in different species. How could you help yourself to remember the features these processes have in common and the features they do not?

11.2 Gas exchange in humans

1 Describe the relationship between the heart and the lungs in humans. Refer in your answer to as many named blood vessels as you can.

2   Scientists investigated how a change in the concentration of carbon dioxide in inhaled air affects two factors: the volume of each breath and the breathing rate.

The results of this investigation are shown in Figure 11.1.

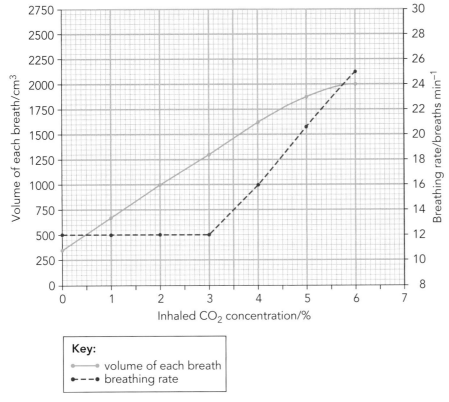

Key:
•——• volume of each breath
•– –• breathing rate

Figure 11.1

a   Describe the effect of increasing the carbon dioxide concentration
    of inhaled air on the:

    i   volume of each breath   [2]

    ii   breathing rate.   [2]

b   Explain the results of this study.   [4]

c   Compare the composition of inspired and expired air.
    Explain the similarities and differences in content.   [2]

                                                            [Total: 10]

3   Complete the sentences with the missing words:

During inhalation, the diaphragm .... and flattens. At the same time, the
.... intercostal muscles contract. These actions increase the ....
of the thorax, which reduces the pressure inside the thorax. Air moves into the lungs.

During exhalation, the diaphragm relaxes and returns to a .... shape.
At the same time, the internal intercostal muscles .... These actions
decrease the volume of the thorax, which increases the ....
inside the thorax. Air is forced out of the lungs.   **[Total: 6]**

≪ RECALL AND CONNECT 2 ≪

Think back to Chapter 2: Cells. Which cells have the greatest surface area to volume ratio? Why is this important?

REFLECTION

Use an analogy to help you remember the structures and activities of the gas exchange system. How could you interpret the model shown in Figure 11.2 to help you? Why does the model not accurately represent gas exchange in humans?

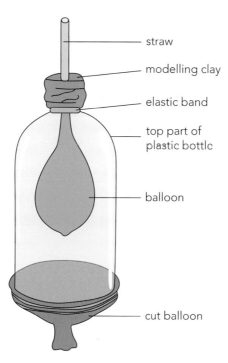

straw

modelling clay

elastic band

top part of plastic bottle

balloon

cut balloon

Figure 11.2: A model of the human gas exchange system

REFLECTION

Did you remember to make a note of the number of marks on offer and time yourself answering the exam-style questions in this chapter? Are you covering all of the marking points in an appropriate amount of time? If not, what strategies could you use to help you improve?

SELF-ASSESSMENT CHECKLIST

Let's revisit the Knowledge focus and Exam skills focus for this chapter.

Decide how confident you are with each statement.

Now I can:	Show it	Needs more work	Almost there	Confident to move on
outline how the body uses energy and how aerobic and anaerobic respiration supply this energy	Draw a mind map to show the different uses of energy by cells.			
recall the equations for aerobic respiration and anaerobic respiration	Write out the various equations that show the different types of respiration.			
describe how gas exchange happens in the lungs and the features of gas exchange surfaces	Draw a diagram that shows how gas exchange surfaces in humans are adapted to their function.			
investigate the differences in composition between inspired and expired air	Design an investigation to compare the differences in composition between inspired and expired air.			
explain the differences in composition between inspired and expired air	Construct a table with two columns, with 'inspired' as the heading of the left column and 'expired' on the right. Fill your table with information relating to the contents of the gases and brief explanations of any changes.			
explain how breathing happens	Draw a flow chart to show the events that cause breathing.			
explain how activity affects breathing rate	Produce a fishbone diagram that shows how physical exercise affects breathing rate.			
distribute time across the whole paper.	Work out how many minutes you have per mark in each paper and time yourself when you answer exam-style questions.			

12 Coordination and response

You practised answering multiple-choice questions in Chapter 10 and synoptic questions in Chapter 8. You have also practiced lots of short-answer questions. In this chapter, you will practise planning and structuring long-form responses. When you attempt these questions remember to plan your response and then structure your writing to ensure there is a beginning, a middle and an end. Dividing your work into these three parts can help produce a response that is as comprehensive as possible.

Some questions – usually describe and/or explain questions – ask you to 'compare' something. You should use comparative words such as 'more', 'less' or terms such 'faster', 'bigger' or 'longer lasting'. Or you may be asked to compare by commenting on similarities and differences.

12.1 The human nervous system

≪ RECALL AND CONNECT 1 ≪

A neurone is an example of a specialised cell. Can you remember four other specialised cells you reviewed in Chapter 2: Cells?

UNDERSTAND THESE TERMS

- stimulus
- nerve impulse
- motor neurone
- relay neurone

1 The nervous system coordinates responses to changes in the internal or external environment of the body.

    a What are the two main parts of the nervous system?

    b Draw a diagram of a motor neurone.

    c What is the function of the myelin sheath?

2 Our body contains many neurones that can communicate with each other.

    a What is the name of the junction between two neurones?

    b How does the nerve impulse cross from one neurone to another at these junctions?

    c You have seen the importance of interlocking molecules before when looking at enzymes and antibodies. How is it important in this context?

3 When a person steps on a pin, they will experience a withdrawal reflex in their foot, preventing damage to the tissue.

    a State the order of the three neurones involved in a reflex arc. [3]

    b Identify where the receptor and effector for this reflex arc are located. [2]

    c Describe and explain two features of reflex actions that make them useful to humans. [4]

[Total: 9]

12.2 Sense organs

1 The eye is a sense organ that transforms light energy into nervous impulses that can be interpreted in your brain.

    a State the names of the two receptor cells for light and state the part of the eye in which they are found. [3]

    b State what happens to the size of a person's pupil when they enter a brightly lit room coming from a dark corridor. [1]

    c Explain how the pupil changes size to control the amount of light that enters it. [4]

[Total: 8]

UNDERSTAND THESE TERMS

- sense organ
- accommodation

2 The eye is one of the main sense organs in the body. It gathers light and sends this to the brain to be interpreted.

a Draw a diagram of the eye with the following structures labelled: retina, optic nerve, cornea, lens, pupil and iris.

b Which two components of the eye refract light?

3 The light of the eye needs to be focused on the part of the retina with the most cone cells.

a State the part of the retina that contains the most cone cells and state the process used to allow light from distances to be focused here. [2]

b Explain how the suspensory ligaments help control this process. [4]

[Total: 6]

12.3 Hormones

1 Hormones are produced throughout the body.

a Name the hormones produced by these glands:

   i adrenal gland [1]

   ii ovary. [1]

b Describe the effects caused by the hormone produced by the adrenal gland. [3]

[Total: 5]

UNDERSTAND THESE TERMS
• hormones
• target organ

2 a How are hormones carried to their target organs?

b What are the effects of insulin?

c Which hormone works in the opposite way to insulin?

3 The body uses the nervous system and the endocrine system to coordinate responses.

a Describe the similarities and differences between the actions of the nervous and endocrine systems. [4]

b Suggest why a reflex action is controlled by the nervous system rather than the endocrine system. [2]

[Total: 6]

REFLECTION

In Question 3a in this section did you mention both the nervous system and the endocrine system at each mark point? These questions suit themselves to a bullet point approach. Can you rewrite your answer more clearly?

12.4 Coordination in plants

<< RECALL AND CONNECT 2 <<

Plant growth hormones move through the plant by diffusion and some
of the processes that cause the growth response require active transport.
What is the difference between diffusion and active transport?

UNDERSTAND
THIS TERM

- tropism

1   Plants respond to their environment to maximise their growth.

  a   Describe an experiment to investigate the effect of the direction of light
      on the growth of shoots.   [6]

  b   Explain what a control experiment is and what your control would
      be in this experiment.   [3]

                                                                        [Total: 9]

2   a   How do shoots and roots compare in their responses to light and gravity?
          Use the correct terminology!

  b   How do these differing responses help the plant survive?

3   Plants respond to different environmental factors by using different tropic
    responses.

  a   Name the hormone that controls tropic responses.   [1]

  b   State the location where this hormone is made and its effect on cells.   [2]

  c   Describe how distribution of this hormone changes when light shines
      from one side and explain what happens.   [3]

                                                                        [Total: 6]

REFLECTION

How did you find the long-form questions? What techniques could you use
to plan and structure your long-form responses? For example, for a question
asking you to identify the differences and similarities between testosterone and
oestrogen, you could use a Venn diagram. Is this something that you think could
work for you? Can you think of other techniques?

SELF-ASSESSMENT CHECKLIST

Let's revisit the Knowledge focus and Exam skills focus for this chapter.

Decide how confident you are with each statement.

Now I can:	Show it	Needs more work	Almost there	Confident to move on
outline the human nervous system	Make a list of the main components of the central and peripheral nervous systems.			
find out how different types of neurones are involved in reflex actions	Sketch and label a reflex arc.			
outline the structure of the eye, as an example of a sense organ	Draw and label the structure of the eye. Can you describe the function of all components?			
find out about hormones and compare nervous and hormonal control in humans	List the four endocrine glands, the hormones they produce (including glucagon in Supplement) and the function of each hormone.			
recall tropic responses in plants	Describe what happens to the root and shoot of a germinating bean, planted underground and explain how it is controlled.			
describe how nerve impulses cross a synapse	Sketch a synapse and label the different components with their names and functions.			
explain how the eye focuses light	Describe what happens to the lens as you move from reading a book to looking into the distance.			
plan and structure long-form responses	List the techniques you could use to plan and structure responses to long-form questions.			
use comparatives to identify or comment on similarities and/or differences where necessary.	Write a question and mark scheme on this topic that requires a comparison – give it to a friend to answer and mark their work.			

13 Excretion and homeostasis

You practised at synoptic questions in Chapter 8: Transport in plants. Remember that synoptic questions require you to consider your knowledge, in broad terms, to link ideas and concepts from different topics together to construct a meaningful response to a question that requires higher-order thinking skills. Before you start answering a question like this, make a brief list of the topics you have studied in the past that have content that overlaps with the current topic. Can you spot the synoptic questions in this chapter?

Questions with the 'give' command word require a short answer, which is usually a word(s) or a statement.

| Give | produce an answer from a given source or memory. |

13.1 Excretion

1 Excretion is one of the seven characteristics of life.
Describe what is meant by the term 'excretion'.

2 Figure 13.1 is a simplified diagram showing the relationship between a human kidney and surrounding blood vessels. Vessel **1** is the aorta.

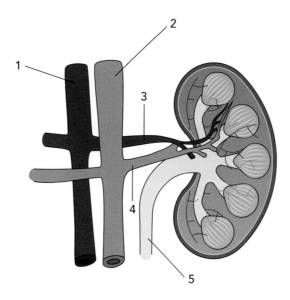

Figure 13.1

a Identify the vessels labelled **3**, **4** and **5**. [3]

b State two differences between the blood in vessels **3** and **4**. [2]

c Vessel **5** contains a fluid.

   i State the name of the organ to which this fluid will be passed. [1]

   ii Give three substances contained in this fluid. [3]

   iii For one of the substances you have identified, describe why it is not returned to the bloodstream. [1]

[Total: 10]

3 Sketch a nephron and label its components. **[Total: 2]**

> **UNDERSTAND THESE TERMS**
> - deamination
> - kidney
> - nephron
> - urea
> - urine

13.2 Homeostasis

1 Copy and complete the following sentences using appropriate terms:

In humans, carbohydrates such as .... can be digested into sugars such as .... These molecules are absorbed into the .... and are carried to cells for the process of ....

2 Figure 13.2 shows a process involved in homeostasis.

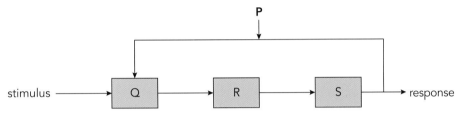

Figure 13.2

a Give the name of the process shown in Figure 13.2. [1]

b Make two copies of the flow diagram shown in Figure 13.2.

    i On your first flow diagram, replace 'stimulus' with 'sugary meal'. Suggest terms for **Q**, **R** and **S** to show how an appropriate response occurs to maintain homeostasis. [4]

    ii On your second flow diagram, replace 'stimulus' with 'cold shower'. Suggest terms for **Q**, **R** and **S** to show how an appropriate response occurs to maintain homeostasis that involves the flow of blood to the skin. [4]

c Adrenaline is a hormone that can be involved in both processes you considered in **b**.

    i Describe what is meant by the term 'hormone'. [1]

    ii Give two effects of adrenaline on the human body. [2]

[Total: 12]

3 Copy and complete the table below to compare nervous and hormonal control, limited to speed of action and duration of effect.

	Speed of action	Duration of effect
Hormonal control		
Nervous control		

[Total: 2]

≪ RECALL AND CONNECT 2 ≪

Describe two ways in which glucose is used in the human body.

UNDERSTAND THESE TERMS

- adrenaline
- diabetes
- endocrine
- glucagon
- hormone
- insulin

REFLECTION

Did you spot the synoptic questions in this chapter? How can you prepare for synoptic questions? You may find mind maps a useful technique – can you think of any others that may work better for you?

SELF-ASSESSMENT CHECKLIST

Let's revisit the Knowledge focus and Exam skills focus for this chapter.

Decide how confident you are with each statement.

Now I can:	Show it	Needs more work	Almost there	Confident to move on
outline the main excretory products of humans and where they are lost from the body	Construct a mind map to show the main excretory products of humans. Add branches to each component to show where they are lost from the body.			
describe homeostasis	Write two or three different definitions of homeostasis that are all correct.			
find out how the kidneys excrete urea and other waste substances	Produce a fishbone diagram that shows how the kidneys excrete urea and other waste substances.			
explain how negative feedback is involved in the maintenance of constant blood glucose concentration and body temperature	Construct simple flow charts to show the process by which negative feedback is involved in the maintenance of constant blood glucose concentration and body temperature.			
understand how to answer synoptic questions better	Identify synoptic questions in this chapter and create a spider diagram showing how the topics link together.			
understand how to answer questions with the 'give' command word.	Check your answers to the 'give' questions in this chapter and the rest of the book. Did you provide a suitable amount of information for each one?			

Exam practice 4

This section contains past paper questions from previous Cambridge exams, which draw together your knowledge on a range of topics that you have covered up to this point. These questions give you the opportunity to test your knowledge and understanding. Additional past paper practice questions can be found in the accompanying digital material.

The following question has an example student response and commentary provided. Once you have worked through the question, read the student response and commentary. Are your answers different to the sample answers?

1   Fig 1.1 is a diagram of the human gas exchange system.

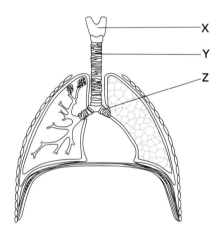

Fig 1.1

a   i   Identify the parts of the gas exchange system labelled **X**, **Y** and **Z**
            in Fig 1.1.   [3]

      ii   State the name of the tissue that prevents the collapse of **Y** and **Z**
            during breathing.   [1]

b   Breathing involves the movement of the ribs and the diaphragm.
      Describe the process of **inspiration**.   [4]

c   State the name of the gas exchange surface in the lungs.   [1]

                                                                                    [Total: 9]

Cambridge IGCSE Biology (0610) Paper 42 Q5, June 2022

Example student response	Commentary

1 a i   X = larynx.
 	
     Y = trachea.
 	
     Z = bronchus.
	This response correctly identifies all three parts of the gas exchange system labelled X, Y and Z in Fig 1.1.
	 This answer is awarded 3 out of 3 marks.

ii Trachea	This is not an acceptable answer and cannot be awarded the mark. The correct answer is cartilage. *This answer is awarded 0 out of 1 mark.*
b The ribs contract while the diaphragm contracts. This increases the pressure in the thorax, which results in air moving into the body from outside.	Although the student has correctly identified that the diaphragm contracts, which is awarded one mark, the ribs do not contract; instead, the external intercostal muscles attached to the ribs contract. Also, the student incorrectly states that the pressure increases in the thorax to facilitate inspiration; however, the opposite is true. *This answer is awarded 1 out of 4 marks.*
c Alveolus	This is the expected answer. *This answer is awarded 1 out of 1 mark.*

Now you have read the commentary to the previous question, here is a similar question that you should attempt. Use the information from the previous response and commentary to guide you as you answer.

2   The gas exchange system is one of the organ systems of the human body.

Fig 2.1 shows parts of the gas exchange system during breathing in and breathing out.

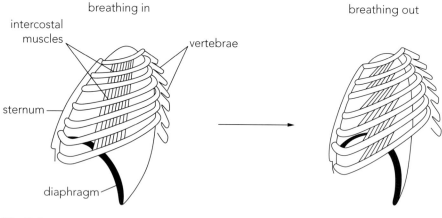

Fig 2.1

a   Complete Table 2.1 to show:

i   the functions of the diaphragm and the intercostal muscles during breathing in and breathing out

ii   the pressure changes in the thorax.

Use these words:

contract   **relax**   **increases**   **decreases**

	diaphragm	intercostal muscles		pressure change in the thorax
		internal	external	
breathing in				
breathing out				

Table 2.1

[4]

Fig 2.2 shows part of the gas exchange surface of a human.

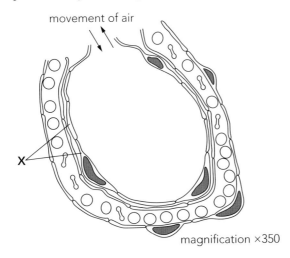

movement of air

X

magnification ×350

Fig 2.2

b   State **two** features of the gas exchange surface that are **visible** in Fig 2.2.   [2]

c   The cells labelled **X** on Fig 2.2 form a tissue.

i   Define the term *tissue*.   [2]

ii   Cartilage is another tissue found in the gas exchange system. State the functions of cartilage in the gas exchange system.   [2]

[Total: 10]

Cambridge IGCSE Biology (0610) Paper 41 Q1, June 2020

The following question has an example student response and commentary provided. Once you have read and answered the questions, read the student response and commentary and compare your answers. Are your answers different? If so, how are they different?

3   a   Fig 3.1 shows the change that occurs in the eye after it is exposed to bright light.

before exposure   after exposure

Fig 3.1

Describe the change to the eye in Fig 3.1 **and** explain why this change is important.   [3]

   b   The eye is a sense organ.

The skin is another type of sense organ.

State **two** stimuli that the skin responds to.   [2]

[Total: 5]

Cambridge IGCSE Biology (0610) Paper 32 Q1b-c, November 2021

Example student response	Commentary
3 **a** The iris contracts and gets smaller. This protects the eye from too much light.	**a** The pupil constricts as a result of the circular muscles of the iris contracting. The statement 'the iris contracts' is incorrect. The second statement is correct if imprecise and lacking in detail. It also does not include an explanation as to why this is important. *This answer is awarded 1 out of 3 marks.*
b Temperature and touch	**b** These are correct. *This answer is awarded 2 out of 2 marks.*

4   Now write an improved answer to parts of Question 3 where you did not score highly. Use the commentary to guide you as you answer.

The following question has an example student commentary and answer provided. Work through the question first, then compare your answer to the sample answer and commentary.

5   Two identical potted plants were used to investigate plant responses. Plant **A** was placed on a clinostat that continually rotated. Plant **B** was not rotated. Both plants were then placed on their sides and kept in the dark. Fig 5.1 shows the two plants at the start of the experiment and after seven days.

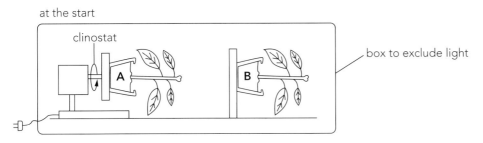

Fig 5.1

a   State the name of the response shown by the shoot of plant **B**.   [1]

b   Explain the reason for constantly rotating plant **A**.   [2]

c   i   State the name of the plant hormone that causes the response of the shoot of plant **B**.   [1]

   ii   Explain how the plant hormone causes the response of plant **B**.   [3]

d   Seeds germinate in the soil. The seedlings that grow from seeds show the same response as shown by plant **B** in Fig 5.1. Explain the advantages of this response to the survival of seedlings and mature plants.   [3]

[Total: 10]

Cambridge IGCSE Biology (0610) Paper 41 Q4, June 2021

Example student response	Commentary
5 a Tropism	This is a tropic response but it should specifically be gravitropism. *This answer is awarded 0 out of 1 mark.*
b It makes it a fair test so that you can compare the response with plant B.	The phrase 'fair test' should not be used at this level. The comparison gains one mark but to get the second mark, the student should have mentioned that this set-up will negate the effect of gravity on the shoot. *This answer is awarded 1 out of 2 marks.*
c i Auxin **ii** Auxin osmoses from the top to the bottom of the plant where it builds up. This causes the stem to grow upwards.	**c i** Correct, scoring one mark. *This answer is awarded 1 out of 1 mark.* **ii** Osmosis is only used for water so the student should have used diffused (or even moved). It would be best if they had also discussed cell elongation on this lower side of the stem. *This answer is awarded 2 out of 3 marks.*
d The plant needs light for photosynthesis so the stem grows towards the light.	This statement is correct but the student needs to look at the marks available and ensure their answer matches this. They could have included the requirement of carbon dioxide for photosynthesis, oxygen for respiration or access to pollinators for the flowers. This question calls back to some of the earlier plant chapters. *This answer is awarded 1 out of 3 marks.*

Now you have read the commentary to the previous question, here is a similar question that you should attempt. Use the information from the previous response and commentary to guide you as you answer.

6 Involuntary actions occur because nerve impulses travel along the components of reflex arcs.

An example of an involuntary action is the rapid movement of a hand after unexpectedly touching a very hot object.

Fig 6.1 shows the structures that are involved in the movement of the hand.

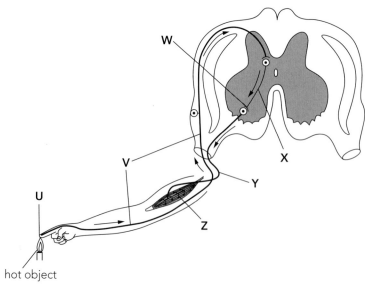

Fig 6.1

Table 6.1 shows the functions of some of the structures shown in Fig 6.1, the names of the structures and the letter from Fig 6.1 that identifies each structure.

a   Complete Table 6.1.

function	name	letter on Figure 6.1
conducts impulses to central nervous system (CNS)		
conducts impulses to an effector		
conducts impulses only within the CNS		
	receptor	
		Z

Table 6.1

[5]

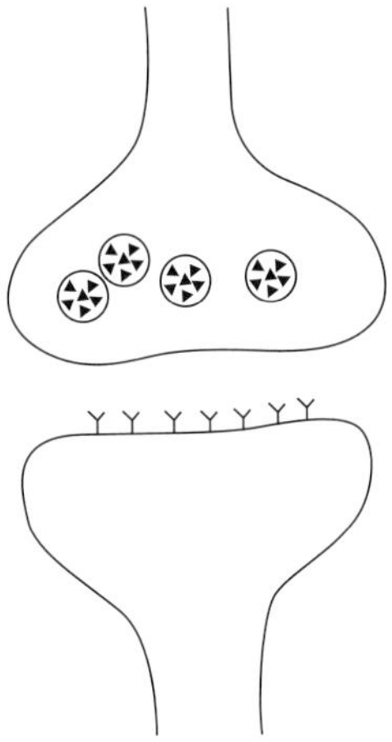

Fig 6.2

b   Fig 6.2 shows the structure of the synapse at **W** on Fig 6.1.
    Describe how an impulse travels across the synapse shown in Fig 6.2.   [4]
c   State **one** example of a reflex action that occurs in the eye.   [1]

[Total: 10]

Cambridge IGCSE Biology (0610) Paper 42 Q4, November 2021

This question has an example student commentary and answer provided. Work through the question first, then compare your answer to the sample answer and commentary. Are your answers different to the sample responses? What information does this give you about your understanding of the topic?

7   Fig 7.1 shows a section through a kidney.

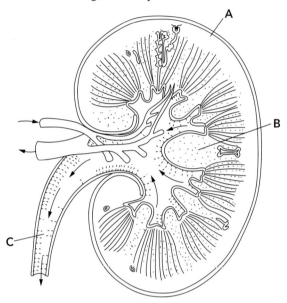

Fig 7.1

a   Complete the table by stating the name of the parts labelled **A**, **B** and **C** on **Figure 7.1**.

letter	name of part
A	
B	
C	

[3]

b   i   Name the blood vessel in Fig 7.1 that has the highest concentration of urea.   [1]

ii   Name the blood vessel in Fig 7.1 that has the lowest concentration of glucose.   [1]

c   Explain the role of the kidney in excretion.   [4]

[Total: 9]

Cambridge IGCSE Biology (0610) Paper 42 Q3a–c, November 2016

Example student response	Commentary
7 a 	letter	name of part	 	A	medulla	 	B	cortex	 	C	urethra		The student has mistaken the medulla for the cortex and vice versa. The part labelled **C** is the ureter, not the urethra. *This answer is awarded 0 out of 3 marks.*
b i C	This is the expected answer. *This answer is awarded 1 out of 1 mark.*
ii C	This is the expected answer *This answer is awarded 1 out of 1 mark.*
c The kidney is an organ that filters blood to remove all toxins, including drugs and urine. Some salt is also removed from the blood, also some water that is not needed by the body. The kidney achieves this using nephrons.	The student does not refer to the process of filtration in the kidney in any substantial detail. However, one mark can be awarded for the reference to filtering of the blood, as well as excess water. *This answer is awarded 2 out of 4 marks.*

Now you have read the commentary to the previous question, here is a question on a similar topic that you should attempt. Use the information from the previous response and commentary to guide you as you answer.

8   The kidneys filter blood, separate useful molecules from excretory wastes and control the water content of the blood.

Fig 8.1 is a diagram of a kidney tubule and associated blood vessels. The arrows show the direction of blood flow.

Fig 8.2 is a drawing of a vertical section through a cell from the lining of region 2 of the tubule.

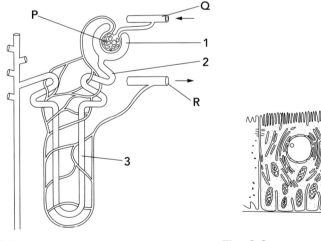

Fig 8.1   Fig. 8.2

a i State the name of structure **P**. [1]

    ii Blood vessel **Q** has the highest blood pressure. Suggest why. [1]

    iii The structures labelled **S** on Fig 8.2 are microvilli. Explain the importance of the microvilli on the surface of these cells. [2]

b Table 8.1 shows the concentrations of some substances in blood plasma and in the regions labelled 1 and 3 on the tubule shown in Fig 8.1.

substance	concentration/mg per cm^3		
	blood plasma	region 1	region 3
protein	8000	0	0
glucose	100	100	0
salts	320	320	300
urea	30	30	2000

Table 8.1

Outline how the kidney tubules function to produce urine from the substances in blood plasma. Use the information in Fig 8.1, Fig 8.2 and Table 8.1 to support your answer. [6]

c The kidneys are examples of organs that help the body to maintain a constant internal environment.

    i State the term for maintaining a constant internal environment by negative feedback. [1]

    ii Explain how negative feedback controls the blood glucose concentration of a person who has **not** eaten for a day. [3]

[Total: 14]

Cambridge IGCSE Biology (0610) Paper 42 Q2, June 2022

14 Reproduction in plants

The questions in this chapter contain a variety of command words. You must look carefully at the command word – if you are asked to explain the shape of a graph, for example, you will not gain marks if you simply describe it (even if your description is perfect!). Similarly, a valid answer for a question that has the 'suggest' command word where you're expected to come up with a new interpretation of the material then this will not gain you the marks on a state or define question which is looking for the specific material covered in the syllabus.

This chapter also contains a 'define' question. 'Define' questions require a definition of a key word, term or process. Make sure your definitions are correct (and precise) by learning the definitions given in your Coursebook, or in a copy of the syllabus.

Define	give precise meaning.

14.1 Asexual and sexual reproduction

UNDERSTAND THESE TERMS

- gamete
- zygote
- diploid
- mitosis (Supplement)

1   Different organisms have different ways of replicating. Some organisms replicate asexually, others sexually and some can do both depending on the circumstances.

   a   What is asexual reproduction and how is it different from sexual reproduction?

   b   What are three different ways that organisms can reproduce asexually using a specific example for each?

   c   What is an advantage and a disadvantage of asexual reproduction?

2   Sexual reproduction involves two individuals and male and female gametes.

   a   What is a gamete and what is the main difference between a gamete and a typical cell in an organism?

   b   Why is the difference essential to ensuring healthy offspring after fertilisation?

   c   What is the name of the process that produces gametes in sexually reproducing organisms?

3   Figure 14.1 shows a strawberry plant. It can reproduce sexually through the gametes it produces in its flowers and asexually through the formation of runners.

Figure 14.1

   a   Define the term 'sexual reproduction'.   [1]

   b   Explain why asexual reproduction is useful in a crop plant such as a strawberry.   [3]

   c   The number of chromosomes in a leaf cell of a strawberry is 56. State the number of chromosomes in a pollen cell and explain its importance.   [3]

                                                                            [Total: 7]

14.2 Sexual reproduction in flowering plants

UNDERSTAND THIS TERM

- pollination

1   Flowers, like the one shown in Figure 14.2, are the sexual organs of plants and are adapted to this purpose.

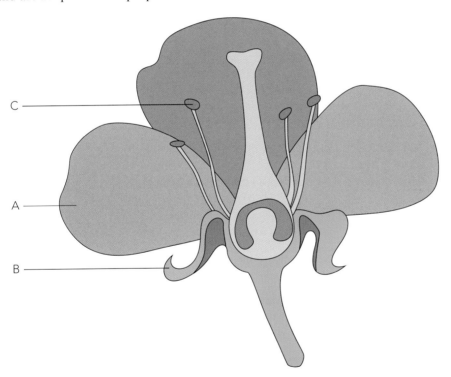

Figure 14.2

a   State the name of the parts of the plants labelled in the diagram.   [3]

b   Describe the structure of the female part of the flower.   [4]

c   Explain how the structure of an insect-pollinated flower is adapted to increase the likelihood of pollination.   [4]

[Total: 11]

2 Plants can be pollinated by pollinators such as insects or bats and by the wind.

    a How is the structure of pollen from a wind-pollinated plant different to that of an insect-pollinated plant?

    b What are the differences between the anthers and stigmas of these two types of plants?

3 Many flowers have both female and male parts that can produce both types of gamete.

    a State the term that describes the process when a pollen grain from a plant lands on its own stigma. [1]

    b Suggest and explain a way that a plant can prevent this from occurring. [3]

    c Explain what happens to the pollen grain once it lands on the stigma leading up to fertilisation. [3]

[Total: 7]

14.3 Advantages and disadvantages of different methods of reproduction

1 Many plants can reproduce sexually and asexually.

    a Explain the advantages of a plant reproducing asexually rather than sexually. [4]

    b Suggest when a plant may reproduce asexually. [1]

[Total: 5]

2 **a** What is the difference between self-pollination and cross-pollination?

    b How is self-pollination different to asexual reproduction?

3 Sexual reproduction is found in many multicellular organisms, including plants.

    a Explain why the offspring from sexual reproduction are not identical. [3]

    b Suggest and explain why asexually reproducing crop plants are more at risk of a novel disease than sexually reproducing plants. [2]

[Total: 5]

REFLECTION

Look back at your answer to Question 3b, which has the common 'suggest and explain' command word combination. The 'suggest' command word is looking for information that is not directly learnt but you should be able to get to or deduce from your knowledge, which you will then use to answer the 'explain' part of the question. Did your answer cover both command words? What techniques could you employ during an exam to make sure you don't forget to answer any command words in questions that contain more than one?

SELF-ASSESSMENT CHECKLIST

Let's revisit the Knowledge focus and Exam skills focus for this chapter.

Decide how confident you are with each statement.

Now I can:	Show it	Needs more work	Almost there	Confident to move on
outline the differences between sexual and asexual reproduction	Create a flow chart showing sexual and asexual reproduction with the numbers of chromosomes inside the cells.			
find out how flowers are involved in sexual reproduction	Sketch and label a typical insect-pollinated flower and write down the function of each of the labelled parts.			
investigate seed germination	Write a plan for an investigation to test which conditions are required for germination.			
outline self- and cross-pollination and their potential effects on a population	Make a table comparing asexual reproduction, self-pollination and cross-pollination.			
understand how to answer questions with the 'define' command word	Write a definition for all of the key terms in the orange 'Understand these terms' boxes in this chapter. Compare them to the Coursebook definitions to check your accuracy.			
recognise command words in instructional text.	Choose three questions from Exam practice 3 and highlight all the command words you can identify in the questions.			

15 Reproduction in humans

Examiners write questions with a specific answer in mind, which they provide in a mark scheme. The closer you are to the mark scheme answer, the more likely you are to gain full marks. There are lots of strategies to help achieve this, such as structuring your answer in a logical manner (for example, following a chronological progression such as the reflex arc) and by using the correct terminology throughout.

Get into the habit of comparing your answers to the ones provided to check what a model answer looks like.

The commentary in the Exam practice sections will also help you to understand what good answers look like.

15.1 The human reproductive systems

1 Why are the structures of a human sperm cell and a human egg cell different from each other?

2 Figure 15.1a shows the human reproductive systems and Figure 15.1b shows a flow diagram that features terms associated with reproduction. Use both figures to help you answer the following questions.

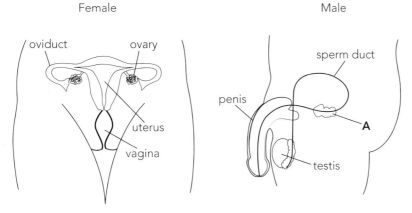

Figure 15.1a: The human reproductive systems

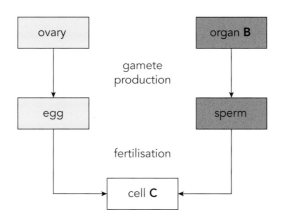

Figure 15.1b

a Identify the organ of the male reproductive system labelled **A** in Figure 15.1a and state its function. [2]

b Identify organ **B** in Figure 15.1b and state a function, other than producing sperm. [2]

c Describe the events that occur after the final stage in the flowchart in Figure 15.1b that result in the formation of an embryo from cell **C**. [4]

d Copy the diagram and draw a line labelled **D** on Figure 15.1.b to show the position of the placenta in a pregnant female. [1]

[Total: 9]

3 The placenta has an important role in human reproduction.
Describe the functions of the placenta in humans. **[Total: 3]**

4 Describe the differences between the roles of oestrogen and progesterone
in the menstrual cycle. **[Total: 2]**

> ### « RECALL AND CONNECT 1 «
>
> Look back at Chapter 2: Cells. How are the sperm and egg cells in humans
> adapted to their roles in achieving successful reproduction?

UNDERSTAND THESE TERMS
• reproduction
• sperm
• egg
• placenta
• oestrogen
• progesterone

5 How are the substances and cells produced by the ovaries and testes similar?
How are these substances and cells different?

> ### REFLECTION
>
> Do you feel confident that you know what a good answer should look like?
> Consider how you structure your answers and compare them to the ones
> provided. Once you have identified where your answers differ and have corrected
> your work, try to answer the questions again fully in a couple of days' time.
> Do you notice a difference in the marks you gained the second time around?

15.2 Sexually transmitted infections

> ### « RECALL AND CONNECT 2 «
>
> Look back at Chapter 10: Diseases and immunity. Define the term
> 'infectious disease'.

1 Copy and complete the following sentences using appropriate terms.

A .... (STI) is an infection that can
be transmitted through .... contact. One example of an STI is caused
by the .... immunodeficiency .... (HIV). Infection with
HIV can lead to ....

2 Figure 15.2 shows how the number of white blood cells and virus particles changes in the blood of an individual who was infected by HIV.

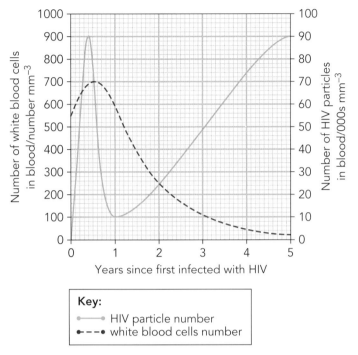

Figure 15.2

a Describe how the number of HIV particles changes within the first year of infection (0–1 years). [2]

b Describe and suggest an explanation for the relationship between the number of white blood cells and the number of virus particles more than one year after infection. [3]

c Suggest one reason to explain why the graph shown in Figure 15.2 would not be identical for every person infected with HIV. [1]

[Total: 6]

3 Construct a simple mind map to show the methods of transmission of HIV and then expand on each of these ideas by including additional items to show how the spread of HIV can be controlled (some control methods will apply to the same method of transmission).

4 What is an STI?

REFLECTION

How confident do you feel that you understand the relationship between HIV and AIDS? What could you do to increase your confidence?

UNDERSTAND THESE TERMS

- sexually transmitted infection (STI)
- human immunodeficiency virus (HIV)
- AIDS

SELF-ASSESSMENT CHECKLIST

Let's revisit the Knowledge focus and Exam skills focus for this chapter.

Decide how confident you are with each statement.

Now I can:	Show it	Needs more work	Almost there	Confident to move on
recall the structure and function of the male and female reproductive systems	Add labels to unlabelled diagrams of the male and female reproductive systems. For each of your labels, write a short sentence to describe its function.			
understand how sperm and egg cells are adapted for their functions	Create sketches to show the adaptive features of egg and sperm cells and provide explanations for each of them.			
describe how hormones are involved in reproduction	Create Venn diagrams to show the similarities and differences between the sites of production and the functions of the hormones involved in the menstrual cycle and pregnancy.			
explain that HIV is a sexually transmitted infection	Design a simple pamphlet or infographic to summarise how HIV is transmitted and how its transmission can be controlled.			
identify what a good answer looks like and practise writing your own.	Compare your answers to the questions in this book to the mark scheme and see how you can improve.			

16 Chromosomes, genes and proteins

KNOWLEDGE FOCUS

In this chapter you will answer questions on:

- chromosomes and cell division
- inheriting genes

> **genes and protein synthesis.**

EXAM SKILLS FOCUS

In this chapter you will:

- evaluate your progress and understand what to do next to improve.

It is important to regularly evaluate your progress as you work through your course. This will help you to identify topics and skills that you feel confident about and those where more revision or practice is required. For each topic, you should identify any holes in your knowledge. Focus your revision on filling those holes, rather than reviewing topics you are more familiar with. It is also good practice to check your understanding of the exam command words – this chapter contains a variety of different command words, so is a good opportunity for you to make sure you know what is required for each. Further support for revision is given in the Exam skills chapter.

16.1 Chromosomes and cell division

<< RECALL AND CONNECT 1 <<

In Chapter 14: Reproduction in plants you saw the importance of meiosis and mitosis in sexual and asexual reproduction respectively. Why was it important that meiosis was used to generate the gametes used in sexual reproduction?

UNDERSTAND THESE TERMS

- gene
- allele

1   Organisms look the way they do and can produce specific proteins in their cells because of the genetic information stored within their cells.

   a   How is genetic information stored within the nucleus of eukaryotic cells?

   b   What is the relationship between the terms DNA, gene and allele?

   c   Why are humans different to each other even though they have the same number of chromosomes and the same genes?

2   Mammals reproduce via sexual reproduction, requiring the use of meiosis to produce the gametes.

   a   A skin cell of a tiger (*Panthera tigris*) has 38 chromosomes. How many chromosomes does an egg cell of a tiger have?

   b   Why is meiosis described as a reduction division?

3   All cells in the body of an animal have the same genetic information.

   a   State the form of cell division that leads to genetically identical offspring.   [1]

   b   Describe what needs to occur in the cell before it can replicate.   [2]

                                                [Total: 3]

4   Explain why cells produced by mitosis are different from the ones produced by meiosis.   **[Total: 3]**

REFLECTION

Have a look at the answers provided to the previous questions and review your progress. Do you find that structuring your answers comes easier to you now? Are there still command words that you find tricky? If there are, this is a good opportunity to practise those questions with those command words to ensure you are fully prepared before your exams.

16.2 Inheriting genes

1 Polydactyly is a dominant genetic condition that is controlled by a single gene and results in a phenotype where an individual has six fingers and toes on each of their hands and feet. Polydactyly is coded for by the allele **A** and the non-mutated allele (for five fingers and toes) is coded by the allele **a**.

a State the two genotypes that will lead to a phenotype showing polydactyly. [2]

b An individual who is heterozygous for the polydactyly allele has a child with a person with five fingers. Construct a genetic diagram to show this cross and state the ratio of the offspring that are likely to show polydactyly. [4]

c Suggest and explain a way to determine, by looking at their offspring, whether or not an individual is homozygous or heterozygous for **A**. [3]

[Total: 8]

> UNDERSTAND
> THESE TERMS
>
> • heterozygous
>
> • phenotype

2 Blood groups are coded for by three different alleles, I^A, I^B, I^o. An individual with the genotype I^AI^B will have the blood group **AB**.

a What is the name of this type of inheritance where both alleles are visible in the phenotype?

b What is the ratio of the phenotypes in the offspring of an individual with blood group **AB** and an individual with blood group **O**?

c Why do traits that are found on the sex chromosomes show different inheritance patterns than those that are found on any of the other chromosomes?

3 Cats have the same names for the sex chromosomes as humans (XX is female and XY is male). The gene for coat colour for cats is X-linked. X^A codes for orange fur and X^B codes for black fur.

a State the genotype of a male, black cat. [1]

b A female cat with the genotype X^AX^B is calico, a mixture of black and orange fur. Explain how this has occurred. [2]

c A female, calico cat mates with a black male cat. Determine the ratio of offspring produced, using a Punnett square in your answer. [3]

[Total: 6]

16.3 Genes and protein synthesis

« RECALL AND CONNECT 2 «

In Chapter 4: Biological molecules, you saw the structure of DNA.
Can you describe its structure and how it is held together?

1   Different cells in the body will look different even though they have the same genetic material in their nucleus.

a   Explain how different cells end up with different proteins, while having the same genetic material.   [3]

b   Describe the process of protein synthesis.   [4]

c   Ricin is a toxin produced by the castor oil plant (*Ricinus communis*). Ricin inactivates the function of ribosomes in cells. Suggest and explain why this toxin is fatal if not treated within the first few days of exposure.   [3]

[Total: 10]

UNDERSTAND THIS TERM
• expressed

2   Multicellular organisms have specialised cells that are adapted to carry out specific functions.

a   What is the name of the cells in the human embryo that can still turn into any other type of cell?

b   What is an example of the type of cell described in **a** that still exists in your body?

c   How do these cells change into different specialised cells?

3   Proteins are made in all cells and carry out a wide range of functions.

a   What smaller organic molecules are proteins made up of?

b   What determines the order of these smaller organic molecules in the protein chain?

c   What is the role of mRNA in protein synthesis?

REFLECTION

It is important to have base knowledge that you can apply within the context of exam questions. For example, in Question 1c in this section you are expected to know the function of the ribosomes, even if you have not heard of ricin before. If you lack the base knowledge of protein synthesis, then you will not be able to apply it. Were you able to apply this knowledge correctly in this context? What could you do to help you identify any areas where you have gaps in your knowledge?

SELF-ASSESSMENT CHECKLIST

Let's revisit the Knowledge focus and Exam skills focus for this chapter.

Decide how confident you are with each statement.

Now I can:	Show it	Needs more work	Almost there	Confident to move on
understand about chromosomes and genes	Draw a diagram to show that chromosomes contain genes and that genes come in different forms called alleles.			
use genetic diagrams to predict how characteristics are inherited	Write down the ratios produced by the various types of cross covered in this chapter (e.g. dominant/recessive, codominant, sex-linked).			
find out about how and why cells divide by mitosis and meiosis	Draw a flow diagram of mitosis and meiosis and label this with the key similarities and differences.			
understand how genes determine the proteins that are made in a cell	Make a video where you describe the process of protein synthesis.			
evaluate progress and understand what to do next to improve.	Make a list of sections in this book where you have ticked 'Needs more work' or 'Almost there'. Make a revision plan to go over these topics.			

17 Variation and selection

When answering questions, you need to decide whether your answer needs to be short, detailed or structured, or whether you need to include calculations or specific units. The command words in a question will help you choose what form your answer will take and if you need to include specific units or biological terms. This chapter will provide opportunities for you to practise answering questions with different command words, which will require different forms of answers.

17.1 Variation

1 Which part of a human cell contains a chemical substance that partly controls the features of the organism? What is this chemical substance called?

2 Human red blood cells are normally biconcave in shape.
However, in some people, red blood cells become sickle-shaped. Figure 17.1 shows the shape of normal red blood cells and sickle red blood cells.

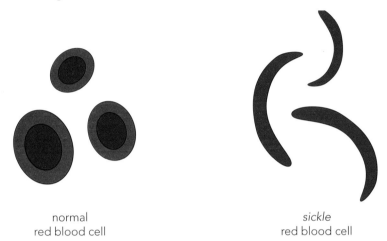

normal
red blood cell

sickle
red blood cell

Figure 17.1

a The sickle shape of the red blood cells in Figure 17.1 is caused by a gene mutation.

    i Define the term 'gene mutation'. [1]

    ii State one factor that increases the rate of mutation. [1]

b There is variation in the shape of human red blood cells.

    i State a type of variation shown by the shape of human red blood cells. [1]

    ii Explain your answer to **i**. [1]

c Apart from mutation, state one other source of genetic variation in human populations. [1]

[Total: 5]

3 Suggest an advantage of mutations. **[Total: 1]**

> ## ≪ RECALL AND CONNECT 1 ≪
>
> Look back at Chapter 16: Chromosomes, genes and proteins. Continuous and discontinuous variation have genetic and environmental causes. However, which of these is generally most responsible for each type of variation?

UNDERSTAND THESE TERMS

- continuous
- discontinuous
- mutation
- selection
- variation

17.2 Selection

1   Describe the process of natural selection.

2   The peppered moth (*Biston betularia*) is preyed upon by birds.
    It can exist in two forms, **P** and **Q** (Figure 17.2).

Figure 17.2

a   The colour of the peppered moth is an adaptive feature.
        Explain the term 'adaptive feature' with reference to these colours.   [2]

b   Figure 17.3 shows the changes in the population size of moths
        of type **P** and type **Q** during a period of 200 years.

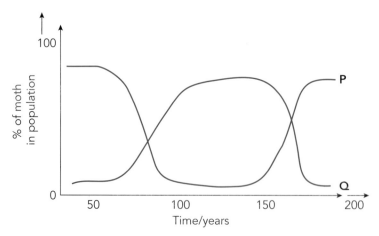

Figure 17.3: The change in population of two types of peppered moth
(*Biston betularia*) over a period of 200 years

UNDERSTAND
THESE TERMS

- adaptation
- artificial selection
- natural selection
- selective breeding

At various times during this period, the level of air pollution in this environment changed, which led to moths of type Q being better suited to their environment.

    i   State a time at which air pollution was highest.   [1]

    ii   Explain the pattern of the two populations of moths shown in Figure 17.3.   [3]

c   Describe **two** ways in which natural selection is different to artificial selection by selective breeding.   [2]

[Total: 8]

3   Copy and complete the following sentences using appropriate terms:

In a population of bacteria, by chance, one may have a .... that makes it .... to an antibiotic. Antibiotic is added, which .... most bacteria. However, a few will .... and form a population of bacteria just like itself.

≪ RECALL AND CONNECT 2 ≪

Look back at Chapter 2: Cells. Describe one way in which a red blood cell in the human body is adapted to its function.

SELF-ASSESSMENT CHECKLIST

Let's revisit the Knowledge focus and Exam skills focus for this chapter.

Decide how confident you are with each statement.

Now I can:	Show it	Needs more work	Almost there	Confident to move on
find out about discontinuous and continuous variation and what causes them	Construct a simple mind map to show the different features of continuous variation and of discontinuous variation, including examples.			
identify and describe adaptive features in different species	Write a simple definition of what an adaptive feature is and draw simple labelled sketches of xerophytes and hydrophytes to show how they are adapted to their environments.			

CONTINUED

Now I can:	Show it	Needs more work	Almost there	Confident to move on
think about how selection can cause changes in the features of a species or population	Create a flow chart to show how populations of bacteria resistant to antibiotics have arisen by natural selection and draw a Venn diagram to show the similarities and differences between natural and artificial selection.			
recognise high-quality responses to questions.	For any questions where you lost marks, analyse the reason. Was it a gap in your knowledge, misreading the question or the level of detail in your answer? Use this to improve your answers.			

Exam practice 5

This section contains past paper questions from previous Cambridge exams, which draw together your knowledge on a range of topics that you have covered up to this point. These questions give you the opportunity to test your knowledge and understanding. Additional past paper practice questions can be found in the accompanying digital material.

The following question has an example student response and commentary provided. Once you have worked through the question, read the student response and commentary. Are your answers different to the example response?

1   A scientist investigated sexual reproduction in flowering plants. Fig 1.1 shows the procedure for crossing two plants of the same species.

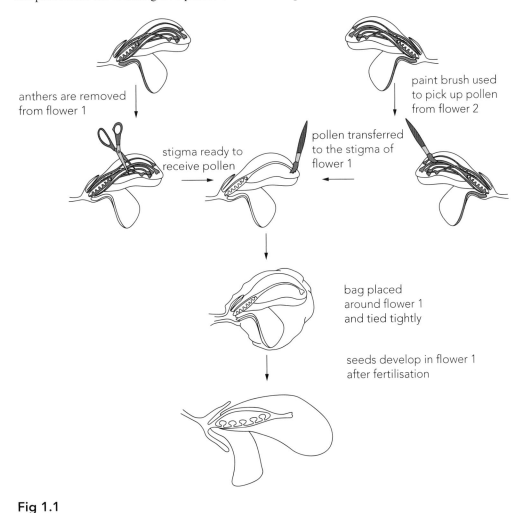

anthers are removed from flower 1

paint brush used to pick up pollen from flower 2

stigma ready to receive pollen

pollen transferred to the stigma of flower 1

bag placed around flower 1 and tied tightly

seeds develop in flower 1 after fertilisation

Fig 1.1

The scientist collected the seeds and germinated them. The leaves and flowers of the offspring plants showed phenotypic variation as they were not all identical to the parent plants. The scientist then investigated the chromosomes of all the offspring plants and found that they had exactly the same number of chromosomes as the parent plants.

a   Suggest why the scientist placed a bag around flower 1.   [1]

b   Explain how sexual reproduction results in the variation that the scientist discovered in the offspring plants.   [2]

c   The chromosome number of the offspring plants is the same as the chromosome number of the parent plants in this investigation.
Explain how the chromosome number is maintained from one generation to the next.   [2]

[Total: 5]

Cambridge IGCSE Biology (0610) Paper 42 Q2aii–iv, November 2021

Example student response	Commentary
1 a To stop the pollen from falling out.	This is incorrect as the pollen will stick to the stigma. The correct answer should reference that the bag prevents further pollination of the plant. *This answer is awarded 0 out of 1 mark.*
b The pollen and ovule fuse at random so it is not always the same combination of chromosomes.	This is correct but could have been phrased more clearly. The student could have also referred to meiosis and the random separation of chromosomes during this process, with different chromosomes containing different alleles. *This answer is awarded 2 out of 2 marks.*
c It is maintained so that the number of chromosomes does not double with every replication.	This is incorrect as the student has not read the question correctly. The question asks *how* the number of chromosomes is maintained, not *why*, which is what the student answers. *This answer is awarded 0 out of 2 marks.*

2   The student failed to answer part **c** correctly in the above example due to misinterpreting the question. Did you make the same mistake? If so, use the commentary to improve your answer.

Here is a similar question that has an example student commentary and answer provided. Work through the question first, then compare your answer to the sample answer and commentary. Are your answers different to the sample responses? What information does this give you about your understanding of the topic?

3 Fig 3.1 shows how several strawberry plants can be formed from one parent plant.

parent plant

offspring

Fig 3.1

a Explain the type of reproduction that produces plants by the method shown in Fig 3.1. [3]

b Explain the **disadvantages** of the type of reproduction shown in Fig 3.1. [3]

[Total: 6]

Cambridge IGCSE Biology (0610) Paper 42 Q2, November 2018

Example student response	Commentary
3 a This is asexual reproduction because the plants will all be the same.	The student gains one mark for stating asexual reproduction but fails to gain any further marks for the explanation. They should have talked about the plant being *genetically identical* rather than the same, as plants with the same genes will not look exactly the same due to interactions with the environment. They should also have used the term 'mitosis' when describing the method of reproduction. *This answer is awarded 1 out of 3 marks.*

Example student response	Commentary
b Asexual reproduction has disadvantages such as very little genetic variation meaning that nothing new can happen.	The student failed to take heed of the marks available and only stated one disadvantage rather than three. Other disadvantages that could have been included are: Plants compete with each other when reproducing in this manner as they're close together. No new adaptive features (this was hinted at in the answer but not in sufficient detail to warrant a mark). No ability to respond to environmental changes. *This answer is awarded 1 out of 3 marks.*

Now you have read the commentary to the previous question, here is a similar question that you should attempt. Use the information from the previous response and commentary to guide you as you answer.

4 **a** Fig 4.1 is a half-flower drawing of pride of Barbados, *Caesalpinia pulcherrima*.

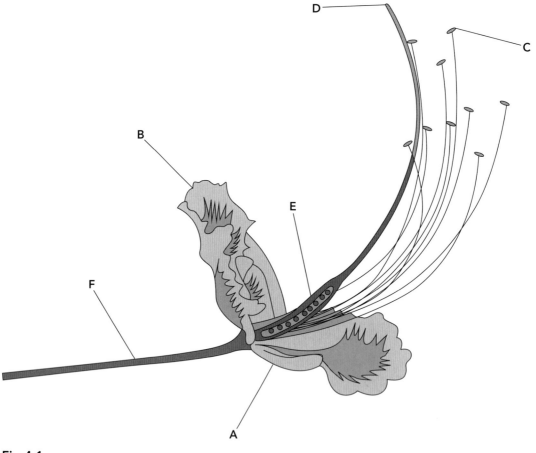

Fig 4.1

Complete Table 4.1 by stating the letter from Fig 4.1 that indicates the organ where each function occurs and the name of the organ. [4]

function	letter from Fig 4.1	name of the organ
meiosis to produce pollen grains		
pollination		
development of seeds		
protection of flower in the bud		

Table 4.1

b Pollen grains grow tubes, which contain haploid male gamete nuclei.

   i   One of these male gamete nuclei fuses with the female gamete. State the part of the flower that contains the female gamete. [1]

   ii Define the term *haploid nucleus*. [1]

   iii Explain why it is important for gametes to be haploid. [1]

[Total: 7]

Cambridge IGCSE Biology (0610) Paper 43 Q6a, c, June 2018

Now attempt the following past paper question. Compare your answer to the commentary and sample answer provided and identify how you could improve your answer. What information does this give about your understanding of this topic as a whole?

5 Fig 5.1 shows the changes in the concentrations of the hormones FSH and LH during a menstrual cycle.

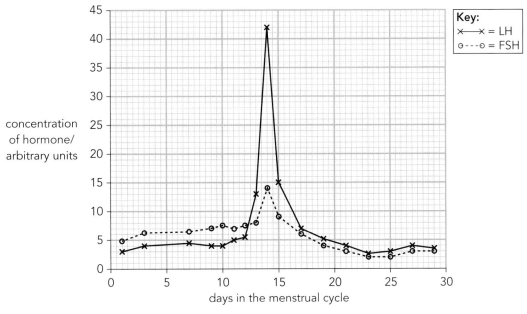

Fig 5.1

a   i   Suggest the target organ for FSH.   [1]

    ii   State how FSH reaches its target organ.   [1]

    iii Describe the relationship shown by the two hormones in Fig 5.1.   [2]

b   Describe the roles of FSH and LH in the menstrual cycle.   [4]

c   Describe the changes that occur in the lining of the uterus during one
    menstrual cycle.   [3]

d   Oral contraceptives are a method of birth control taken by women.
    Outline how the hormones in contraceptives act as a method
    of birth control.   [3]

[Total: 14]

Cambridge IGCSE Biology (0610) Paper 42 Q3, November 2021

Example student response	Commentary
5 a i The brain	FSH is produced in the pituitary gland at the base of the brain, it acts on the ovary. *This answer is awarded 0 out of 1 mark.*
ii It moves there through the blood because it is a hormone.	This is the expected answer. *This answer is awarded 1 out of 1 mark.*
iii They change in similar ways during the menstrual cycle. When one of them rises, the other one rises. When one of them falls, the other one falls.	This student has correctly identified that the two hormones follow the same pattern: an increase, followed by a decrease. However, no additional information is provided and the student cannot achieve any further credit. This would have been possible if there had been a reference to the day at which the two hormones peak in concentration, or some description that included a comparison of the two concentrations. *This answer is awarded 1 out of 2 marks.*
b FSH is follicle stimulating hormone. It causes an ovum to grow in the ovary, once per menstrual cycle. LH is luteinising hormone. It causes the ovum to leave the ovary at the middle of the menstrual cycle (ovulation).	This response correctly identifies the role of FSH in promoting the growth of an ovum. However, no further roles for FSH are included. The student also correctly identifies that LH is involved in promoting ovulation but the response does not expand upon this point. *This answer is awarded 2 out of 4 marks.*
c At the beginning of the menstrual cycle, the uterus lining gets thicker. This is because the ovum, if fertilised, will need to attach so that it can grow. If no fertilised egg attaches, then menstruation happens at the end of the cycle. This involves the loss of the lining of the uterus (mostly blood) via the vagina.	Although the student correctly identifies the growth of the uterus lining at the start of the menstrual cycle, their reference to the breakdown of the lining at the end of one cycle is not creditable here. *This answer is awarded 1 out of 3 marks.*

Example student response	Commentary
d Progesterone in the contraceptive pill can stop ovulation from happening.	This response correctly identifies progesterone as the hormone in contraceptive pills and identifies its role in preventing ovulation. However, the student does not explain how progesterone achieves this. *This answer is awarded 2 out of 3 marks.*

6 Now you have read the commentary, write an improved answer to the sections where you lost marks. Use the commentary to guide you as you improve your answers.

The following question has an example student commentary and answer provided. Work through the question first, then compare your answer to the sample answer and commentary.

7 Colour blindness can be caused by a mutation in a gene. The gene is located on the X chromosome. Fig 7.1 is a pedigree diagram of a family which has several people who are colour-blind.

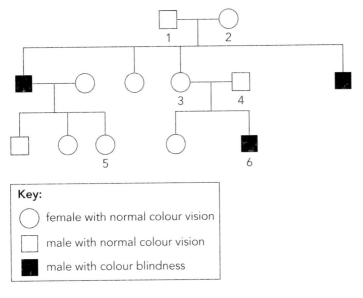

Key:
◯ female with normal colour vision
☐ male with normal colour vision
■ male with colour blindness

Fig 7.1

a Colour blindness is sex-linked. State the evidence from Fig 7.1 that supports the idea that colour blindness is sex-linked. [1]

b State the genotype of person 5.
Use the symbols X and Y for the sex chromosomes and **A** for the dominant allele and **a** for the recessive allele of the gene for colour blindness. [2]

c   Use the information in Fig 7.1 to complete the genetic diagram to show the probability of person **3** and person **4** having another child with colour blindness.

	person **3**	person **4**
parental phenotypes	Female with normal colour vision	Male with normal colour vision

parental genotypes ....

gametes   ( ) ( )   +   ( ) ( )

offspring genotypes ....

offspring phenotypes ....

probability of a child having colour blindness .... [5]

[Total: 8]

Cambridge IGCSE Biology (0610) Paper 42 Q3c, June 2022

Example student response	Commentary
7 a Only males are colour-blind and no females are colour-blind	This answer is correct. Even though you can't guarantee that this means that the trait is sex-linked it does give strong evidence in favour of it being sex-linked. *This answer is awarded 1 out of 1 mark.*
b Aa	This student has not referenced the X or Y chromosomes in their answer. The answer should be X^AX^a. *This answer is awarded 1 out of 2 marks.*
c Person 3 genotype: Aa Person 4 genotype: AA Gametes A/a and A/A Offspring: 50% AA and 50% Aa	The person 3 genotype would get the student the mark even if X^AX^a would be better. They got the genotype for person 4 incorrect as this person is male so would only have an A allele and a Y chromosome. The rest is correct considering their error in the genotype for person 4 and would gain them the mark even though the answer is incorrect. *This answer is awarded 4 out of 5 marks.*

8   The student failed to answer Question **7c** correctly in the above example as they gave the wrong genotype for person 4. Did you answer the question correctly and calculate the correct ratio of offspring generated? If not, use the commentary to improve your answer.

The following question has an example student response and commentary provided. Once you have read and answered the questions, read the student response and commentary and compare your answers. Are your answers different? If they are, how are they different?

9 Merino sheep in South Africa have high-quality wool with very thin hairs.

Breeders in New Zealand have used selective breeding programmes to improve the wool of their sheep to match the quality of South African wool.

    a Describe the steps that breeders would take to breed sheep that have wool with very thin hairs. [5]

    b Explain how natural selection differs from selective breeding. [3]

[Total: 8]

Cambridge IGCSE Biology (0610) Paper 41 Q1c, d, June 2019

Example student response	Commentary
9 **a** The breeder should select sheep that have wool with very thin hairs from their existing stock of animals. They must put males and females together so that they reproduce and then identify the offspring that have similar features. Then breed these.	This response correctly describes how sheep with fine hair should be selected and crossed, which attracts two marks. The response goes on to correctly state that the offspring with fine hairs should be chosen and that these should be crossed. This is also awarded two marks. However, there is no further information provided. *This answer is awarded 4 out of 5 marks.*
b Natural selection occurs in the wild. Natural selection is usually a slower process.	The student correctly identifies that natural selection is usually a slower process than artificial selection by selective breeding. However, the reference to the 'wild' is a vague statement and cannot be awarded credit. The student ought to have referred to environment or surroundings. *This answer is awarded 1 out of 3 marks.*

10 Now write an improved answer to the parts of Question **9** where you did not score highly. You will need to carefully work back through each part of the question, ensuring that you include enough detail and clearly explain each point. Use the commentary to guide you as you answer.

18 Organisms and their environment

Many long answer or higher-mark exam questions use multiple command words such as 'describe' and 'explain' or 'suggest' and 'explain'. Full marks are only awarded when both command words are covered in the answer. There are some of these questions in this chapter. Make sure you cover both command words in your answers to gain full marks.

18.1 Energy flow and ecosystems

<< RECALL AND CONNECT 1 <<

In this chapter we will be mentioning a number of different organisms.
Look back at Chapter 1: Characteristics and classification of living organisms.
What are the five kingdoms of life? Name three classes of vertebrates from
the animal kingdom.

1   Ecosystems consist of the living and non-living environments within a particular
    area. Ecosystems can be large or small depending on what you are looking at.

    a   What is the difference between the terms 'community' and 'population'
        within an ecosystem?

    b   How does energy enter an ecosystem?

    c   How does the energy that enters the ecosystem transfer to a secondary
        consumer such as a fox?

UNDERSTAND THESE TERMS
• niche
• trophic level

2   A savannah ecosystem contains the following food chain:

    grass → wildebeest → leopard

    a   For every 1000 kJ that enters this food chain in the grass, only 10 kJ will
        eventually end up as biomass in the leopard. Where does the rest go?

    b   Why does the loss of available energy as you move up the trophic level limit
        the length of a food chain and the number of top predators?

    c   Why does a pyramid of energy show this better than a pyramid of numbers
        or biomass?

3   Amur leopards (*Panthera pardus orientalis*) are large predatory cats found
    in northern China and eastern Russia. One of its main sources of food
    is sika deer, which are grazing herbivores that mainly feed on grass.

    a   Construct a food chain that reflects the information in the passage above.   [2]

    b   State the trophic level of each of the organisms in the food chain.   [2]

    c   Ecologists that sampled the populations in an area with both of these
        animals using camera traps found that there were between 600–800 sika
        deer within the ecosystem and 5–8 Amur leopards. Explain why the
        number of leopards was limited to single numbers.   [3]

[Total: 7]

18.2 Nutrient cycles

《 RECALL AND CONNECT 2 《

Look at Chapter 4: Biological molecules. Proteins contain four main elements. What are they? Which of these four elements is not found in a carbohydrate?

1 The pea plant (*Pisum sativum*) is a legume. Figure 18.1 shows its root nodules that contain bacteria.

   a Describe the relationship between the bacteria in the root nodules and the pea plant. [3]

   b Suggest and explain why farmers rotate plants without root nodules and those with nodules such as pea plants. [3]

   c Describe the action of denitrifying bacteria. [2]

   Figure 18.1

   [Total: 8]

2 Matter cycles within ecosystems with the key examples being the nitrogen and carbon cycles.

   a What are three biological molecules with a carbon backbone? What are two that contain nitrogen?

   b What is the role of decomposers in the carbon cycle?

   c How does carbon mainly move:

   i into biomass

   ii out of biomass?

3 An ecosystem such as a temperate forest cannot survive without decomposers.

   a Explain the role of decomposers in ecosystems. [3]

   b Suggest why matter is recycled but energy can only be transferred in a linear fashion. [2]

   c Suggest and explain one adaptation of plants in a nitrogen-poor soil such as the waterlogged soil in swamps. [3]

   [Total: 8]

> UNDERSTAND
> THESE TERMS
>
> • nitrogen fixation (Supplement)
>
> • nitrification (Supplement)

REFLECTION

You need to ensure that you have three marking points in your answer for 3c in this section. Look back at your answer. Could you give yourself three marks? Have you answered both the suggest and explain parts of the question? If not, how could you extend your answer? Do this with every longer answer you write and you will pick up marks across your exam paper.

18.3 Populations

1 A population of bacteria is added to a liquid medium containing all of the nutrients it requires to grow. The population is sampled at regular intervals with the population estimates detailed in the following table:

Time after bacteria were added/hours	Population estimate/millions
0	2.0
6	2.5
12	6.5
24	20.0
48	15.0

  a Describe the trend in the data in the table. [3]

  b Calculate the rate of increase between 6 and 12 hours. [2]

  c Explain the slow initial increase between 0 and 6 hours. [2]

  d Suggest and explain a reason for the decrease in population numbers between 24 and 48 hours. [2]

[Total: 9]

UNDERSTAND THIS TERM

• exponential phase

REFLECTION

In Question 1d, two command words are used. To gain both marks you need to both suggest and explain your reason. Answering only one aspect of the question will limit the number of marks you can get to. How will you make sure that you notice when two command words are used in a question and structure your answer so both are addressed?

2 The populations of rabbits and stoats in a habitat were measured over time.

  a It was found that the populations barely changed over time. Why do you think this might be?

  b If stoats were removed from the habitat the population of rabbits would initially increase. What would stop them from increasing indefinitely?

  c If stoats were then reintroduced what would happen to the population of both species over the coming years?

3 The human population doubled from 4 billion in 1974 to 8 billion in 2022.

  a What are some of the main reasons for this rapid population growth?

  b South Sudan has one of the highest birth rates in the world (in 2022). This has been the case for the past decade. What shape would the age pyramid for South Sudan look like?

  c Latvia has a negative growth rate. This means more people are dying than are being born. What would Latvia's age pyramid look like?

SELF-ASSESSMENT CHECKLIST

Let's revisit the Knowledge focus and Exam skills focus for this chapter.

Decide how confident you are with each statement.

Now I can:	Show it	Needs more work	Almost there	Confident to move on
explain how energy is transferred through food webs and back to the environment	Create a local food web and identify three food chains within it, stating the organisms' trophic levels.			
practise using pyramids of number and biomass	State the difference between pyramids of number and biomass.			
describe nutrient cycles in ecosystems	Make a flow diagram of the carbon cycle.			
use graphs and diagrams to describe and explain population growth	Draw and label the typical sigmoid population curve.			
explain why pyramids of energy or biomass provide more useful information than pyramids of number	Explain why pyramids of number and biomass are not always pyramidal in shape, whereas a pyramid of energy is.			
practise answering questions containing multiple command words.	Look back at previous exam questions you have covered in this book. Can you spot any more questions with multiple command words? What are the most common combinations?			

19 Human influences on ecosystems

The command word 'determine' requires you to establish an answer using the information available. When you come to the 'determine' question in this chapter, consider underlining the key information and then make sure that you have used all of it when forming your response.

Determine	establish an answer using the information available.

19.1 Human pressures on ecosystems

1   Suggest reasons to explain why threats to biodiversity are very common around the Earth's equator.

2   Consider the list of key terms below:

> fertilisers   selective breeding   agricultural machinery
> insecticides   intensive livestock production
> large-scale monocultures   herbicides

a   State which of these approaches increases crop yield.

b   Identify two approaches that can lead to the pollution of habitats and describe how this can occur.

3   Scientists investigated the levels of pollution of a stream located next to a sewage processing centre. They took five samples of water from the stream at the locations shown in Figure 19.1.

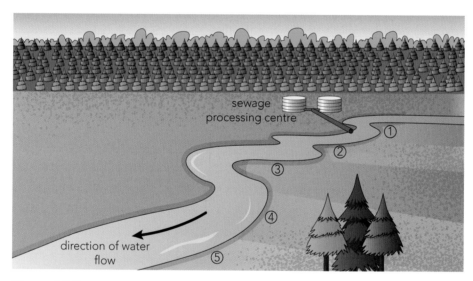

Figure 19.1

The scientists determined:

- The relative concentration of dissolved oxygen at these five sites, relative to the site that had the most dissolved oxygen. This was given the value of 100%.

- The number of bacteria per 100 cm³ of water sampled.

Their results are shown in Table 19.1.

Site	Relative oxygen concentration/%	Number of bacteria per 100 cm³
1	100	230
2	23	152 000
3	34	23 500
4	67	1450
5	88	860

Table 19.1 An investigation into the relative oxygen concentration and bacterial populations in a stream located near a sewage processing centre

a Describe how the number of bacteria shown in Table 19.1 changes as distance increases from the sewage processing plant. [2]

b Suggest the relationship between the relative oxygen concentration and the number of bacteria per 100 cm³. [3]

c State one ion present in sewage that is likely to be responsible for the findings of this study. [1]

[Total: 6]

REFLECTION

Compare your answer to Question 3b in this section with the one provided – do you think your answer would be awarded full marks? Did you miss any key information? How could you make sure that does not happen in the future?

4 Apart from pollution, describe reasons for the reduction of biodiversity in some parts of the world.

《 RECALL AND CONNECT 1 《

Think back to your earlier work on the mineral ion requirements of plants in Chapter 18: Organisms and their environment. What ions are needed? What happens if a plant fails to obtain them?

UNDERSTAND THESE TERMS

- biodiversity
- deforestation
- fertiliser
- monoculture
- pollution

19.2 Conservation

1   Suggest reasons why most of the endangered species are top consumers in food webs.

2   The Philippine eagle, *Pithecophaga jefferyi*, is one of the world's rarest birds.

A survey found that from 540 individuals that lived in 2010, 490 remained in 2016.

a   Calculate the percentage decrease in the population of Philippine eagles during this time. Give your answer to one decimal place. [3]

b   Give **three** reasons why organisms such as the Philippine eagle can become endangered. [3]

Efforts have been made in the Philippines and other countries to increase the numbers of individuals of this species.

c   Describe how endangered species such as the Philippine eagle can be conserved. [3]

[Total: 9]

3   Describe the risks to a species of very low population size.   **[Total: 3]**

4   Using examples in your answer, describe what is meant by the term 'sustainable management'.

UNDERSTAND THESE TERMS
• artificial insemination
• endangered
• extinct
• in vitro fertilisation
• sustainable

≪ RECALL AND CONNECT 2 ≪

Look back to previous chapters and find an example of a percentage yield calculation. What is the formula?

REFLECTION

Conserving endangered species and preventing their extinction is a significant task. Do you feel confident that you could list all the reasons to describe why these efforts are made? How will you check your list? If there are any that you missed, how will you make sure you remember them next time?

SELF-ASSESSMENT CHECKLIST

Let's revisit the Knowledge focus and Exam skills focus for this chapter.

Decide how confident you are with each statement.

Now I can:	Show it	Needs more work	Almost there	Confident to move on
consider how humans have increased food production and how this can affect the environment	Construct a mind map to show how different farming approaches have helped to increase food production and the effects on the environment.			

CONTINUED

Now I can:	Show it	Needs more work	Almost there	Confident to move on
think about why habitats have been destroyed, including deforestation	Write a series of multiple-choice questions (with correct answers) to test a classmate that considers the reasons for habitat destruction, including deforestation.			
outline some examples of pollution and their effects, including climate change	Write questions about: effects of untreated sewage and excess fertiliser on aquatic ecosystems; non-biodegradable plastics on aquatic and terrestrial ecosystems; biodegradable plastics on aquatic and terrestrial ecosystems; the process by which eutrophication is caused and occurs. They should include the command words 'describe' or 'explain'.			
discuss reasons for conservation and some of the things that we can do to conserve species, habitats and ecosystems	Create a Venn diagram to show the similarities and differences between the ways in which forests and fish stocks can be conserved.			
explain that climate change, habitat destruction, hunting, pollution and introduced species can cause species to become endangered or extinct	Construct a mind map that summarises the processes by which species can become endangered or extinct.			
understand how to answer questions with the command word 'determine'.	Write a question with the 'determine' command word on a topic covered in this chapter, along with the mark scheme.			

20 Biotechnology and genetic modification

Exam questions sometimes require you to consider both sides of an argument, such as the benefits and drawbacks of using genetic modification in crop plants. It is good practice to check your answers to this type questions to make sure you have looked at both aspects. Add in the missing part if necessary.

20.1 Biotechnology

1 Microorganisms such as yeast and bacteria are the most commonly used organisms in biotechnology.

   a How can yeast be used to make ethanol for biofuel from sugar cane?

   b What are some of the advantages and disadvantages of using ethanol-based biofuels to power cars?

2 Biological washing powders contain enzymes that can break down stains in clothing. Different enzymes are present to break down different molecules.

   a Egg white is mostly made up of protein. What enzyme would be used to break down egg white stains?

   b Enzymes used in washing powder are mass-produced in fermenters. What are some of the key features of a fermenter that allow it to grow bacteria in large quantities?

   c Why is it important that the nutrient liquid and the fermenter vessel are sterilised prior to use?

3 Figure 20.1 shows yeast (*Saccharomyces cerevisiae*). Yeast is an organism that has had industrial applications for thousands of years.

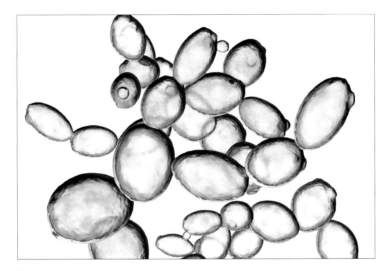

Figure 20.1: Yeast (*Saccharomyces cerevisiae*)

a Yeast will respire anaerobically even in the presence of oxygen. State the word equation for the anaerobic breakdown of glucose by yeast. [1]

b State and explain **two** applications for yeast that have been used for thousands of years. [4]

c Different fungi can produce an enzyme called pectinase. Describe its use in the food industry. [2]

[Total: 7]

20.2 Genetic modification

≪ RECALL AND CONNECT 2 ≪

Proteins are produced in the cell. Outline the process by which the sequence of amino acids in a protein is determined. Look back at Chapter 16: Chromosomes, genes and proteins, to remind you.

UNDERSTAND THESE TERMS

- recombinant plasmid
- DNA ligase

1 Human growth hormone (hGH) is a hormone produced by the pituitary gland that controls growth in children and adolescents. Some people do not produce enough themselves and need a supplemental source of hGH. This used to be extracted from the glands of cadavers, but is now produced by genetically engineered bacteria.

a Describe the process by which a genetically engineered bacterium producing hGH can be produced. [5]

b Suggest **two** reasons why using genetically engineered bacteria is an advantage in this case. [2]

[Total: 7]

2 Genetically modified crops have become commonly used in many countries, including the US. In other areas of the world, such as the EU, their use is restricted.

a What are some advantages of using genetically modified crops?

b Why is their use restricted in some countries?

c Why do you think that genetically modified bacteria are much more widely accepted than genetically modified crop plants?

3 Genetic engineering has allowed scientists to develop crop plants that have novel characteristics such as herbicide resistance.

a State **two** other applications of genetic modification in crop plants. [2]

b Describe whether herbicide resistance is a desirable characteristic in crop plants by evaluating the advantages and disadvantages. [3]

[Total: 5]

REFLECTION

For Question 3b, in this section, did you remember to include at least one benefit and one drawback to genetically engineering crop plants to have herbicide resistance? Do you feel confident you understand how to structure your responses to questions that ask you to evaluate?

SELF-ASSESSMENT CHECKLIST

Let's revisit the Knowledge focus and Exam skills focus for this chapter.

Decide how confident you are with each statement.

Now I can:	Show it	Needs more work	Almost there	Confident to move on
find out how we can use microorganisms and enzymes to make useful products	Give three examples of how yeast and bacteria are used in biotechnology.			
outline some examples of genetic modification	Describe three types of genetically modified crop plants.			
explain how genetic modification is done	Draw a flow chart of the process of genetically engineering a bacterial strain to express a human gene.			
discuss the advantages and disadvantages of genetic modification of crop plants	Make a table listing advantages and disadvantages of crop genetic modification.			
understand how to answer questions that ask you to evaluate sides of an argument.	Topics where you evaluate are often controversial topics, or at least topics to which there are two sides. Go through the syllabus and make a list of other topics that might be suited to evaluation.			

Exam practice 6

This section contains past paper questions from previous Cambridge exams, which draw together your knowledge on a range of topics that you have covered up to this point. These questions give you the opportunity to test your knowledge and understanding. Additional past paper practice questions can be found in the accompanying digital material.

The following question has an example student response and commentary provided. Once you have worked through the question, read the student response and commentary. Are your answers different to the sample answers?

1   Nitrogen is an important element for organisms. In a livestock farm, waste from animals contains protein.

This waste is often spread on farmland as a fertiliser.

Describe how the nitrogen in protein is recycled in the soil into a form that plants can absorb and use.   **[Total: 5]**

Cambridge IGCSE Biology (0610) Paper 42 Q5b, November 2021

Example student response	Commentary
1 The nitrogen in the proteins dissolves in water as nitrates, which can be absorbed through the roots in the plant and the plants can then use them to make new amino acids for their proteins.	This is not a very strong answer. The student references the absorption of nitrates through the roots but demonstrates no understanding of how these nitrates were derived from amino acids in the proteins as part of the nitrogen cycle.
	The student should have included all the steps leading from protein in the waste to nitrates in the soil as well as the organisms involved.
	This answer is awarded 1 out of 5 marks.

2   The student missed out on key segments of the process by which nitrates are produced from protein. Can you write a more complete answer?

The following question has an example student response and commentary provided. Once you have read and answered the questions, read the student response and commentary and compare your answers. Are your answers different? If they are, how are the different?

3   Genetically engineered bacteria that are used to make insulin were grown in a fermenter for five days.

Samples were taken from the fermenter every six hours and the number of bacteria in 1.0 mm³ of the nutrient solution was counted.

Changes in the numbers of living bacteria in the samples taken from the fermenter are shown in Fig 3.1.

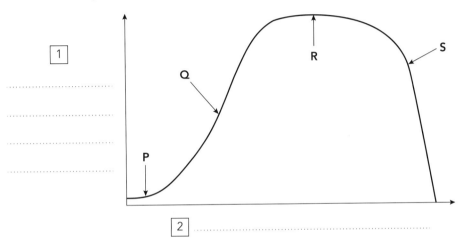

Fig 3.1

i   Complete Fig 3.1 by adding labels for the axes at ☐1 and ☐2.   [1]

ii   State the names of the stages of population growth of the bacteria labelled **P** to **S**.   [2]

iii   Explain, with reference to Fig 3.1, why the bacteria did not grow in the fermenter for longer than five days.   [3]

[Total: 6]

Cambridge IGCSE Biology (0610) Paper 41 Q3c, June 2021

Example student response	Commentary
3 i 1 Number of bacteria 2 Time	The student states the correct label but has not included a unit of volume in the first label (e.g. number of bacteria per mm³). The second label misses a unit (e.g. hours or days). *This answer is awarded 0 out of 1 mark.*
ii P: lag, Q: exponential (log); R: stationary; S: death	These are correct. *This answer is awarded 2 out of 2 marks.*
iii There was not enough food for them to grow and eventually they died.	The student has given one reason but the question has three marks. They should have expanded with further possible reasons such as the build-up of toxins, limited space, lack of oxygen or any other limiting factor. *This answer is awarded 1 out of 3 marks.*

The following two questions are on similar topics. Use the information from the previous response and commentary to guide you as you answer.

4   Fig 4.1 shows part of the nitrogen cycle.

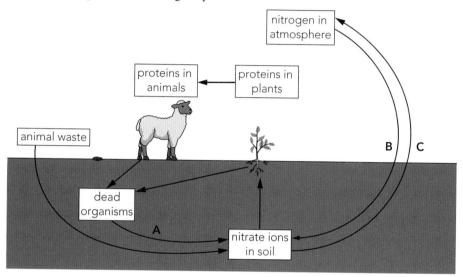

Fig 4.1

a   Describe processes **A**, **B** and **C** in Fig 4.1. [6]

b   State the name of the process that plants use to absorb nitrate ions. [1]

[Total: 7]

Cambridge IGCSE Biology (0610) Paper 42 Q2c, March 2021

5   Fig 5.1 is a food web for some of the microorganisms in a sewage treatment works. *Didinium*, *Paramecium* and *Vorticella* are all examples of protoctists called ciliates.

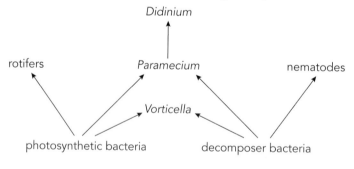

Fig 5.1

a   Construct **one** food chain with three trophic levels that use energy derived from the breakdown of sewage. Do **not** draw the organisms. [1]

b   The water that passed out of the sewage works was often cloudy with suspended matter.

Scientists discovered that ciliates reduce the cloudiness of water during sewage treatment.

Suggest how the ciliates reduce the cloudiness of the water using the information in Fig 5.1. [2]

c   Nitrifying bacteria are found in sewage works. Explain the importance
    of nitrifying bacteria in the nitrogen cycle.   [3]

                                                                    [Total: 6]

Cambridge IGCSE Biology (0610) Paper 41 Q5di, ii, iv, June 2020

Now attempt the following past paper question. Work through the questions first then
compare your answers to the sample answers and commentary. Identify how you could
improve your answers.

6   a   Fig 6.1 is a flow chart showing some of the processes that occur in a biofuels
        power plant.

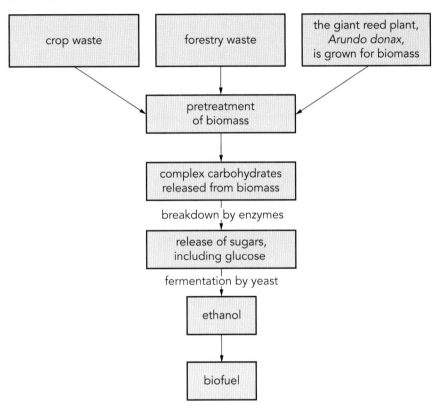

Fig 6.1

    i   The fermentation stage shown in Fig 6.1 requires yeast.

        Complete the balanced chemical equation to show how ethanol is
        produced by yeast respiration.

        .... $\rightarrow$ .... + ...
                                                                            [2]

    ii Using the information in Fig 6.1, suggest the environmental
        advantages of using ethanol as a fuel.   [3]

    iii Farmers grow giant reed plants as monocultures.

        Describe the disadvantages of growing giant reed plants to provide
        biomass for the production of biofuels.   [2]

b One problem with using biomass in the process shown in Fig 6.1 is that the breakdown stage produces a sugar called xylose and ethanoic acid. Yeast cannot use xylose and ethanoic acid is toxic to yeast.

Scientists genetically engineered a type of yeast that can use xylose and ethanoic acid.

Fig 6.2 shows the results of one of the trial experiments done by the scientists using their new genetically engineered yeast.

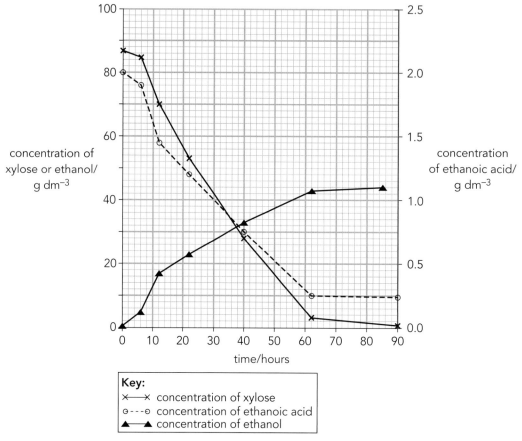

Fig 6.2

i Describe the results shown in Fig 6.2. [3]

ii The experiment was done at 30°C.

The scientists repeated the experiment at 20°C.

Predict the results that you would expect for the concentration of ethanol. [1]

[Total: 11]

Cambridge IGCSE Biology (0610) Paper 42 Q4, November 2022

Example student response	Commentary
6 **a** **i** $C_6H_{12}O_6 \rightarrow C_2H_5OH + CO_2$	The student used the correct formula but failed to balance the equation. Two molecules of ethanol and carbon dioxide are produced for every molecule of glucose. *This answer is awarded 1 out of 2 marks.*
ii It uses waste materials and that means it uses less fossil fuel.	The student gains two marks for this linked statement but needed a third point to ensure full marks for this question. They could have talked about this operation being carbon-neutral or sustainable and having no effect on the enhanced greenhouse effect. *This answer is awarded 2 out of 3 marks.*
iii It is a reed so you have to grow it in water and this can destroy the habitats of water birds.	The student fixated on the term 'reed' and misinterpreted the question as this particular reed grows on land. They gained one mark for stating it was destroying habitats. They could have included that the land could be used for food production or conservation. They could also have looked at it from a monoculture perspective. *This answer is awarded 1 out of 3 marks.*
b **i** As the concentrations of xylose and ethanoic acid decrease, the concentration of ethanol increases. This is because the yeast is breaking down these materials down into ethanol.	The student didn't note the command word 'describe'. They gain their mark for the identification of the correlation but do not gain the further two marks for the reason behind this correlation. *This answer is awarded 1 out of 3 marks.*
ii You would expect less ethanol to be produced in the same time.	Correct. *This answer is awarded 1 out of 1 mark.*

The following two questions are on similar topics. Use the information from the previous response and commentary to guide you as you answer.

7 **a** Insulin produced by genetically engineered bacteria first became available in 1982. Before 1982, insulin had been prepared from dead animal tissues. Explain the **advantages** of using insulin produced by genetically engineered bacteria rather than insulin from dead animal tissues. [3]

b Fig 7.1 shows some of the steps involved in the genetic engineering of bacteria.

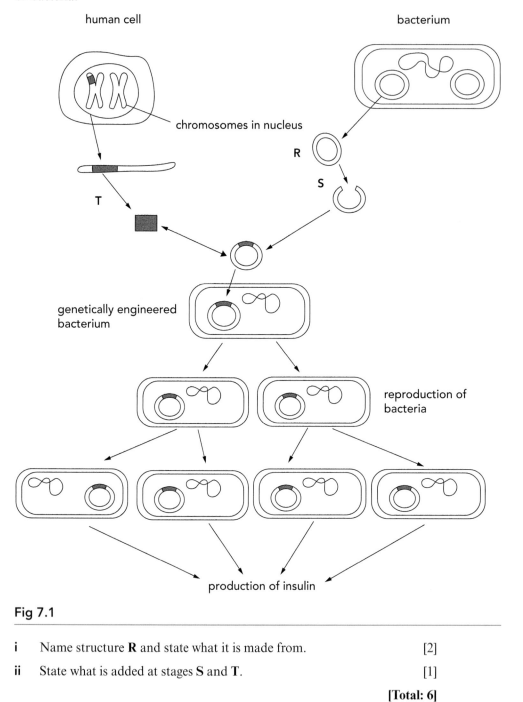

Fig 7.1

i   Name structure **R** and state what it is made from.   [2]

ii State what is added at stages **S** and **T**.   [1]

[**Total: 6**]

Cambridge IGCSE Biology (0610) Paper 32 Q5d, e, November 2009

8 **a** Define the term '*genetic engineering*'. [2]

b Fig 8.1 is a flow diagram that shows how insulin can be produced using genetic engineering.

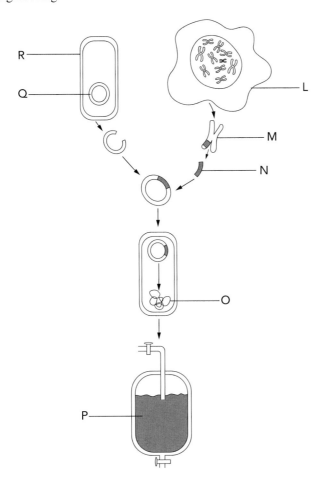

Fig 8.1

Table 8.1 shows stages in the production of insulin by genetic engineering. Complete Table 8.1. The first row has been done for you.

letter from Fig 8.1	name	description
M	chromosomes	threads of DNA found in the nucleus
		section of DNA removed from human cell
	plasmid	
		type of cell that is genetically engineered
		specific chain of amino acids coded by the section of DNA removed from the human cell
	fermenter	

Table 8.1

[5]

c   The genetically engineered cells in Fig 8.1 reproduce asexually.
Explain the advantages of asexual reproduction for insulin production
by genetic engineering.   [3]

[Total: 10]

Cambridge IGCSE Biology (0610) Paper 33 Q6, November 2015

› Acknowledgements

The authors and publishers acknowledge the following sources of copyright material and are grateful for the permissions granted. While every effort has been made, it has not always been possible to identify the sources of all the material used, or to trace all copyright holders. If any omissions are brought to our notice, we will be happy to include the appropriate acknowledgements on reprinting.

Cambridge International copyright material in this publication is reproduced under licence and remains the intellectual property of Cambridge Assessment International Education. Cambridge Assessment International Education bears no responsibility for the example answers to questions taken from its past question papers which are contained in this publication.

Thanks to the following for permission to reproduce images:

Cover Martin Kyburz/EyeEm/Getty Images; *Inside* **Unit 2** Ed Reschke/Getty Images; Steve Gschmeissner/Science Photo Library/ Getty Images; Ed Reschke/Getty Images; **Exam Practice 1** WIM VAN EGMOND/SCIENCE PHOTO LIBRARY; Ed Reschke/Getty Images; **Unit 6** Ed Reschke/Getty Images; **Exam Practice 2** Vladimir Zapletin/Alamy Stock Photo; **Unit 8** Olikim/Getty Images; Steve Gschmeissner/Getty Images; **Exam Practice 3** Oxford Scientific/Getty Images; **Unit 14** Wataru Yanagida/Getty Images; **Unit 17** Ian_Redding/Getty Images; **Unit 18** Tomasz Klejdysz/Getty Images; **Unit 20** Dr_Microbe/Getty Images; **Practical Guidance** Darrell Gulin/Getty Images